Cocoa

Resources series

Cocoa

KRISTY LEISSLE

polity

First published in 2018 by Polity Press

Polity Press
65 Bridge Street
Cambridge CB2 1UR, UK

Polity Press
101 Station Landing
Suite 300
Medford, MA 02155, USA

ISBN-13: 978-1-5095-1316-1
ISBN-13: 978-1-5095-1317-8 (pb)

A catalogue record for this book is available from the British Library.

Names: Leissle, Kristy, author.
Title: Cocoa / Kristy Leissle.
Description: Medford, MA : Polity Press, 2018. | Series: Resources series | Includes bibliographical references and index.
Identifiers: LCCN 2017024116 (print) | LCCN 2017026237 (ebook) | ISBN 9781509513192 (Mobi) | ISBN 9781509513208 (Epub) | ISBN 9781509513161 (hardback) | ISBN 9781509513178 (pbk.)
Subjects: LCSH: Cocoa trade. | Chocolate industry.
Classification: LCC HD9200.A2 (ebook) | LCC HD9200.A2 L45 2018 (print) | DDC
  338.4/766392--dc23
LC record available at https://lccn.loc.gov/2017024116

Typeset in 10.5 on 13pt Scala by
Servis Filmsetting Ltd, Stockport, Cheshire
Printed and bound in the UK by Clays Ltd, St Ives PLC

The publisher has used its best endeavours to ensure that the URLs for external websites referred to in this book are correct and active at the time of going to press. However, the publisher has no responsibility for the websites and can make no guarantee that a site will remain live or that the content is or will remain appropriate.

Every effort has been made to trace all copyright holders, but if any have been inadvertently overlooked the publisher will be pleased to include any necessary credits in any subsequent reprint or edition.

For further information on Polity, visit our website: politybooks.com

Contents

Abbreviations

Note: All spellings are true to organizational usage, here and elsewhere in this volume.

ADM	Archer Daniels Midland
AGOA	African Growth and Opportunity Act (US)
Caistab	Caisse de Stabilisation (Ivory Coast)
CATIE	Centro Agronómico Tropical de Investigación y Enseñanza (Costa Rica)
CBE	cocoa butter equivalent
CCC	Conseil du Café-Cacao (Ivory Coast)
COCOBOD	Ghana Cocoa Board
EPZ	export processing zone
EU	European Union
FCCI	Fine Cacao and Chocolate Institute
FCIA	Fine Chocolate Industry Association
FDA	Food and Drug Administration (US)
FLO	Fairtrade Labelling Organizations International
FOB	free on board
FTZ	free trade zone
GDP	gross domestic product
GH₵	Ghanaian cedis
GNI	gross national income
HCP	Heirloom Cacao Preservation Fund
ICCO	International Cocoa Organization
ICI	International Cocoa Initiative

IITA	International Institute of Tropical Agriculture
ILO	International Labour Office (permanent secretariat of the International Labour Organization)
ILRF	International Labor Rights Forum
IMF	International Monetary Fund
IPEC	International Programme on the Elimination of Child Labour
LBC	licensed buying company (Ghana)
MT	metric tonnes
NAFTA	North American Free Trade Agreement (Canada, Mexico, US)
PBC	Produce Buying Company (Ghana)
PISA	Produits des Iles SA (Haiti)
QBCS	ICCO *Quarterly Bulletin of Cocoa Statistics*
SAP	structural adjustment program
USDA	United States Department of Agriculture
USITC	United States International Trade Commission
WTO	World Trade Organization

Figures and Tables

Acknowledgments

My first thanks go to Louise Knight at Polity for extending the invitation to author *Cocoa* for the Resources series, and to Louise and Nekane Tanaka Galdos for their teamwork and support from proposal to printed volume. I am indebted to the many colleagues and friends who generously gave of their time and expertise, improving this book in innumerable ways. In Seattle, the constant friendship and bountiful knowledge of Lauren Adler and Bill Fredericks started shaping *Cocoa* long before I knew I would write it. In San Francisco, John Kehoe, Gary Guittard, and Amy Guittard welcomed me to Guittard Chocolate Company and shared insights from a family that has worked in the industry for five generations. Greg D'Alesandre at Dandelion Chocolate offered philosophical and practical insights into sourcing. I also thank Molly Gore at Dandelion for her expert engagement with my writing over the years. Dr. Carla Martin and Colin Gasko kindly allowed me to observe a Cacao Grader Intensive workshop, and Carla offered further insights into the work of the Fine Cacao and Chocolate Institute in an interview. From Accra, Priscilla Addison and Kimberly Addison at '57 Chocolate thoughtfully shared their experiences in an email interview. In London, Sophi Tranchell and Charlotte Borger at Divine Chocolate graciously gave interviews and read lengthy portions of the manuscript. I am enormously grateful to Sophi for her unwavering support of my research and writing, starting with my doctoral fieldwork and continuing to this day. Jesse Last at Taza Chocolate, Zohara Mapes Bediz and Laura Sweitzer at TCHO Chocolate, and Hannah Davis and Matt Earlam at Twin & Twin Trading all read portions of the manuscript and gave formative insights into price, quality, and trade justice. I am thankful for thought-provoking conversations with Dr. Jean-Marc Anga and Dr. Michele Nardella at the International Cocoa Organization price risk management workshop in Freetown, as well as a stimulating email exchange with Jane Franch at Numi Organic Tea on the politics of certification. My students in the winter 2016 UWB course, History and Globalization, pushed my thinking with their superb work on the geopolitics of coffee, coltan, diamonds, fish, land, oil, sugar, timber, water – and, of course, cocoa. At crucial moments, Mark Christian and Steve DeVries both read chapters with an immediacy and encouragement that elevated this book in every way. I give thanks for their dedication to advancing our knowledge of cocoa and chocolate. As a scholar with access to a seemingly inexhaustible library system, I have enjoyed many moments of revelation by engaging with English language works on cocoa and chocolate. I have also had the privilege of learning through fieldwork. I thank Hormazd Dastur for opening the door to my earliest work in Ghana, and Tony BouDib, who kept it open even as my departure flight from Accra left the runway. No words are sufficient to thank all the farmers, buyers, managers, graders, depot workers, truck drivers, factory staff, and agricultural officers in Hawaii, Malaysia, Ghana, Ivory Coast, and Sierra Leone who have enlightened and informed me. Among them, I especially thank Percy Yalley for his guidance and mentorship. I was fortunate to complete portions of this manuscript at two writing residencies, and acknowledge Writing Between the Vines, especially founder Marcy Gordon and the staff at Moshin Vineyards, for supporting my time in Sonoma, California, and UW Bothell Interdisciplinary Arts & Sciences, as well as Miriam Bartha, for supporting a residency at the Helen Riaboff Whiteley Center on San Juan Island, Washington. At the latter, I appreciated the company of my UWB colleagues, and particularly thank Rob Trumbull for introducing me to the transformative concept of writing units. I am indebted to three anonymous peer reviewers, whose expertise and insights improved this book immeasurably; any omissions or errors are mine alone. *Cocoa* would never have been in my stewardship were it not for a decisive moment of encouragement, many years ago, from Anita Verna Crofts and Ken Peavler. I hope to show them my gratitude with lasting friendship. Though long hours at a desk sometimes made it feel otherwise, I was never truly alone while writing *Cocoa*. My heart had the constant support of my family of friends, Anita, Ken, Gina, Amy, Memo, Brad, Christopher, Ariella, and Michelle, and of my boundlessly loving family, Denise, Christine, Joe, and Adrienne. Finally, I offer my affectionate gratitude to Gavin, who bore witness to the writing of this book each and every day, always with unconditional love.

CHAPTER ONE

Introduction

When I was about five years old, I tried to run away from home because my mother would not buy me chocolate. I had been watching my cartoons and seen a commercial for Mars's 3 Musketeers. It was bewitching: molten chocolate pouring over a slab of fluffy nougat. I didn't know what nougat was, and I didn't care – it was the glossy, rich, melted chocolate cascading down from an unseen source that captivated me. By that point in my life, chocolate was already my favorite food. I chose it over any other flavor, any other food, at any meal where it was allowed.

But that morning, it wasn't allowed. When I demanded that my mom take me immediately to buy the precious thing I had seen on television, she, not unreasonably, said no. We would have to get the 3 Musketeers another time. But my mind was filled with a vision of drinking the molten chocolate I had seen in the commercial. I suppose I knew the bar would really be solid, but I could still see myself cupping my hands beneath a 3 Musketeers wrapper while liquid chocolate poured forth, and it seemed to me the pinnacle of bliss. When my mother said the chocolate shopping would have to wait, I went into my room, packed some possessions – not money, as I had none – and announced that I was running away. I stomped down the long flight of stairs to the door of our apartment, and let myself outside into the fresh air of upstate New York.

My memory goes blank after that, and I don't remember

how far I got before my mother came to get me – she'd
been watching from the window upstairs. But that image
of molten chocolate has stayed with me. I think of it often,
and the power it had over my young self, strong enough to
make me try and leave home, just to taste it. While my story
may be of an extreme, chocolate has a similar hold over millions of people. We cherish chocolate, we prize and hoard
and savor it. Just the mention of chocolate, especially when
it's unexpected – "Chocolate cake in the office kitchen, help
yourself!" or "It's so chilly today, let's get a hot chocolate"
– can make eyes light right up. But behind every taste of it
lies an industry of many more people who may not share
that same pleasure. For *those* millions, chocolate can mean
a daily grind of tough labor to make a precarious living and,
for the most vulnerable among them, constant suffering.

My five-year-old self had no idea what lay behind that
image of chocolate on the television screen. My adult self
does, after nearly fifteen years of researching this industry.
In this book, I share what I have learned about the global
cocoa trade. Each chapter takes a close look at power relations and politics across the supply chain, from cocoa farms
through the industrial manufacture and retail of chocolate,
with attention to price, quality, justice, and sustainability.
From this introduction through the end of *Cocoa*, I offer
evidence that neither "global," nor "cocoa," nor "trade" has
a sole definition or meaning, fixed by time or place. There
is no single story to tell about the way cocoa is exchanged
around the world. Indeed, every individual who participates
in this industry has her or his own story. And yet many of
these stories share a common narrative about loss or gain,
suffering or pleasure. I analyze how long-lasting industry
structures, as well as new dynamics, shape in powerful
ways who or what benefits from growing, buying, selling,
and manufacturing cocoa, and who or what loses out.

Central to my analysis is the truth that the market is not a neutral entity, bound by laws of nature that only economists can "see." Cocoa markets, just like those for any other good or service, are socially constructed. That is, the exchange of the seeds of *Theobroma cacao* has particular arrangements that differ across geographical contexts and over time. These patterns both reflect and shape the social interactions, hierarchies, and norms of people trading cocoa. Axes of identity that have become meaningful across many societies (though not in the same way or to the same degree), especially gender, race, age, class, nationality, and ethnicity, are integral to cocoa market functions (ability and sexuality also matter, though they are not central analytics in this book). People who are disadvantaged by any of those tend to lose out in the exchange of cocoa, whereas people who are privileged by them tend to win. No matter where you are in the world of growing, selling, buying, transporting, manufacturing, or retailing cocoa, you are more likely to see women – especially young, elderly, widowed, or heads of household – black and brown people, and ethnic minority groups – particularly migrants – suffering, while men, white people, ethnic majority groups, and those with privileged passports gain.

Of course, the same could be said for virtually any market, for any good. I also examine the reverse dynamic: how the specifics of cocoa's husbandry and trade alter, reinforce, or exacerbate social power relations. For example, production scales change dramatically as cocoa moves through the value chain, affording those at the foundation the least economic benefit. More than 90 percent of cocoa comes from smallholders who farm a few hectares of land or less. Because each of the world's five million growers produces only the tiniest fraction of the total crop, they and the millions more who depend upon them live within very tight margins – an economic experience that tends to magnify social inequalities. Because the line between making a living from cocoa and suffering a loss is often very thin, people with any individual sense of power over the crop and its proceeds tend to do what they can to retain it. In this book, I look particularly at how this dynamic plays out in Ghana and Ivory Coast, where cocoa farming has intensified or reinforced the disproportionate suffering of women and migrants.

Moreover, growing cocoa is a long-term investment. It takes three to five years for trees to begin producing fruit, so farmers have a lengthy period during which they must cover growing costs with no income. After that, the cocoa tree is typically productive for about twenty-five years, so it makes economic sense to stick with it. Switching to another export crop is often not feasible for smallholders. Once farmers start growing cocoa – or when they inherit or otherwise come to steward cocoa farmland – they typically become beholden over the long term to the political, economic, and sociocultural powers that govern it. Cocoa's high exit barrier thus contributes to growers' tenacious poverty.

Regional production and export

The cocoa tree, *Theobroma cacao*, is indigenous to Central and South America. Centuries of globalization have spread cultivation across the tree's commercially viable growing zone, which is about 20 degrees north and south of the equator. The result is that, today, most cocoa grows outside the Americas. West Africa is by far the predominant producer region: farmers there grow around three-quarters of all cocoa (see figure 1.1). Ivory Coast, the largest exporter, typically accounts for about 40 percent, Ghana, the second

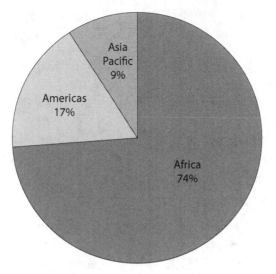

Figure 1.1 Cocoa production by region, 2016–2017 season forecast

Source: International Cocoa Organization (ICCO), *Quarterly Bulletin of Cocoa Statistics (QBCS)*, XLIII, no. 1 (Cocoa Year 2016/17), table 3.

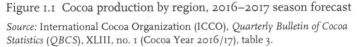

largest, around 20 percent, and Nigeria and Cameroon about 5 percent each. Countries in Central and South America produce less than a fifth of the world total. Thanks mainly to Indonesia, the third largest exporter, Asia Pacific produces about a tenth.

Before the tree moved beyond its indigenous home, and for centuries after it did, cocoa geopolitics looked different to today. Studies of earlier periods necessarily pay close attention to power dynamics within and between Central and South America and the Caribbean, as well as to trade relationships between those regions and Europe and North America, once the latter developed cocoa consumer markets.[1] While I include historical material and contemporary examples from these regions – as well as Asia Pacific – I keep West Africa in the foreground of this book. For more than a century, at least one West African producer has been among the top cocoa exporters, starting with São Tomé and Príncipe, the second largest after Ecuador in 1900.[2] From about 1911, Ghana (then called the Gold Coast) was the leading exporter, a position it retained until Ivory Coast surpassed it in the late 1970s. Today, few countries export large amounts of cocoa, which means supply levels in each of those leading producers matter to industry stability and prospects. Because four of them are in West Africa, the region is a bellwether for, among other things, cocoa's trading price. Market analysts pay constant attention to West Africa's seasonal weather and longer-term climate change, as well as its politics (see chapter 4). These drive how much cocoa the region produces, and how difficult or easy it is to get that cocoa loaded onto container ships and headed to Europe or North America.

As the largest exporter, Ivory Coast's supply is critical. Ghana is important for both supply and quality. Ghana produces the world's best bulk beans, whose flavor is at the heart of what many European and North American consumers know and love as chocolate; its high-grade cocoa thus trades at a premium. Indonesia presents a contrast. While large export volumes make Indonesia important to global supply, most Indonesian cocoa is not fermented – a crucial step for flavor development. Unfermented beans trade at a lower price because they are used as bulk filler, and must be combined with fermented beans to make chocolate.

Though the region is pivotal to contemporary cocoa geopolitics, focusing on West Africa also generates analytical tension. Producers in Central and South America have been growing, trading, processing, and consuming cocoa for millennia – long before the crop reached West

Africa or anywhere else. Their histories and politics, trade routes and cultural practices, shaped human interaction with this fruit and continue to be influential. For example, apart from Ecuador, no country in Central or South America can currently compete with West African export volumes. However, thanks in part to the cultivation of more diverse and rarer beans, cocoa from the Americas and Caribbean is often marked as superior in quality to West African types. I discuss the politics of quality classifications in chapter 7. Here, I point out that, because the country origins of these flavor beans, as they are called, are increasingly named on chocolate packaging, Central and South American and Caribbean countries have disproportionate representation in the consumer context, relative to export volumes. Shoppers are more likely to recognize Venezuela or Trinidad – neither of which exports significant volumes (though both did historically) – as cocoa origins than Cameroon or Nigeria.[3] Another tension has to do with the fact that, across Central and South America, cocoa enters into political economic discussions as a prized consumable. With no history of making anything to drink or eat from the fruit of *Theobroma cacao*, producers and, indeed, governments in Africa and Asia Pacific have tended to emphasize cocoa's importance as an export crop – though they increasingly focus on value-added production (see chapter 3). This export crop identity frames much of my discussion of cocoa geopolitics.

Mapping value

With that in mind, let us take a look at the global economics of cocoa's exchange. In 2016, the value of all traded cocoa was about $12 billion. At the same time, total sales of the finished good that comes from cocoa – chocolate – were about $100 billion. Five companies – Mars, Mondelēz, Ferrero, Nestlé, and Hershey – sell more than half the world's branded chocolate by value (see chapter 4). Their enormous economies of scale mean these companies, and the people who run them, enjoy far higher profit margins than growers. Though they cannot produce *Theobroma cacao* commercially, countries in the Global North enjoy the most economic benefit from cocoa. One way to measure this is to look at grindings, which is the term for processing beans into more usable, and therefore more valuable, forms. As with chocolate makers, major processors are few in number. Just three – Barry Callebaut, Cargill, and Olam – grind nearly two-thirds of the world's beans. Since the turn of the twenty-first century, processing has been expanding in cocoa exporting countries, so much so that, in addition to being the largest cocoa producer, Ivory Coast now has the largest grinding capacity. Despite this shift to Africa-based processing (see chapter 3), Europe remains the leading region. Within it, the Netherlands and Germany grind the most cocoa; outside the European Union (EU) and Ivory Coast, the US has the largest capacity.[4]

Another way of mapping cocoa's economic value is to look at where people eat chocolate. The US leads in total market value. In contrast, African countries are estimated to capture just 2 percent of chocolate's $100 billion world market.[5] Estimates vary in exact amounts, but they generally agree that people in Western European countries – top among them Germany, Switzerland, Ireland, and the UK – consume the most chocolate per person.[6] We can also look at market maturity, or how established chocolate is as a consumable. As historians, anthropologists, and archaeologists have documented, Mesoamerican societies had been putting cocoa beans to a variety of uses for at least three millennia before Europeans encountered them, including as drinks, currency, and ritual accompaniment (see chapter 2).[7] When Europeans did come into contact with cocoa, they needed to learn virtually everything about the novel fruit. Historian Marcy Norton has made the convincing case that, having never seen or tasted anything like cocoa before, sixteenth-century Europeans and their descendants drew upon Mesoamerican knowledge not only to make the drinks, but also to understand why they might want to consume cocoa in the first place.[8] In the nineteenth century, however, there came a shift: technologies of the Industrial Revolution, which began in Britain and spread to continental Europe and North America, made possible a radically new consumable form for cocoa: bar chocolate, which was rectangular, glossy, and sweet, and wrapped in packaging that gave it a brand identity. By virtue of being the earliest to industrialize and mass-produce bar chocolate, North America and Western Europe today are the "mature" chocolate markets.[9]

In these places, bar chocolate assumed an enduring social identity. The companies most successful at crafting this identity, including Cadbury and Hershey, have helped steer consumer desire for chocolate in certain directions – as an affordable luxury, holiday accompaniment, and surrogate for romantic love. Consumers also assert their preferences. Since at least the turn of the twenty-first century, two distinct consumer trends have been apparent in mature markets. One is demand for trade justice along the cocoa supply chain, including better remuneration for farmers and attention to child labor. The result has been a proliferation of bars with ethical trade labels, Fairtrade most prominent among them (see chapter 6). The other has to do with health. Demand is rising for dark chocolate, with its lower sugar content (at least, lower than that of most milk chocolate and bonbons), and for chocolates that claim additional healthy properties, such as "raw" or organic.[10] One market research firm predicted dark chocolate sales will rise almost 9 percent annually through 2019, reaching $51.7 billion – more than half the current value of the chocolate market.[11]

Starting in the late twentieth century, China and India saw fast growth in consumption, giving shoppers there new leverage in how chocolate is sold and marketed.[12] Gifting chocolate, as opposed to buying it for oneself, has emerged as an important aspect in both countries. Both also have large rural populations whose chocolate potential is untapped. Multinational companies are responding with innovations around distribution, packaging, and tech-driven interactive marketing. In contrast to Europe, North America, and new Asian markets, cocoa exporters have low consumption rates for industrial chocolate. While places in Central and South America retain millennia-long practices of consuming cocoa fruit, according to Euromonitor's estimate, the region's 2013 per capita consumption of industrial chocolate confectionery was about a quarter that of Europe and North America. At that time, Asia Pacific had the lowest average chocolate consumption rate – just 0.2 kg (0.44 lb) per capita – with the Middle East and Africa marginally ahead, at 0.3 kg (0.66 lb).[13] Because, historically, consumers in Asia Pacific and Africa have eaten so little chocolate, they have had slight significance as market outlets. Consumer desires in Ghana or Cameroon, for example, have not been an influential force upon the chocolate industry to date. However, this is changing. Overall chocolate demand in mature markets seems to have leveled out, whereas it is growing apace in new ones. For example, in 2013, consumption of chocolate across Africa had risen by more than 50 percent on the decade prior, thanks to a combination of increased local processing capacity, urbanization, and improved infrastructure for distribution and retail. The chocolate market in Nigeria, home to Africa's largest economy, grew 775 percent from 2006 to 2013.[14]

Despite this unevenness in where the economic value of cocoa accrues, dependency characterizes both ends of the supply chain. While processing capacity and consumer markets are rising in some producer countries, these still export most of their crop as a primary agricultural commodity. By and large, the world's five million growers depend upon multinational companies and shoppers overseas to process and consume their crop. On the other hand, some of those multinational companies owe their existence to cocoa. Though two of the three largest processors have diversified product ranges and do not depend exclusively on cocoa, all major processors and manufacturers are headquartered in countries that cannot grow cocoa on a commercial scale.[15] These companies depend on millions of growers, traders, and transportation workers elsewhere – as well as the women and children who provide them with unpaid domestic support – to produce the ingredient they need most. Nor is there a substitute for cocoa. The chemical complexity of the seed and intricacy of chocolate manufacture have meant that, so far, artificial replication of chocolate's flavor has proven impossible. The only "substitute" that appears with any frequency, typically in health food stores, is carob. This legume is indigenous to the Mediterranean region and, it must be admitted, requires some imagination to accept as a chocolate analogue. For the present – and likely forever – cocoa alone can satisfy the desire for chocolate.

Sustainability

With a $100 billion industry and millennia-long history of taste gratification dependent upon its existence, cocoa's sustainability receives a great deal of attention. At the time of writing in mid-2017, the world cocoa crop was abundant, thanks mainly to favorable weather in West Africa. At the same time, demand in mature and new Asian markets had not matched predicted rises. In combination, these factors sent cocoa's price plummeting to a ten-year low. The 2016–17 season is forecast to total over 4.5 million metric tonnes (MT).[16] After grindings, this amount will almost certainly produce a surplus. It would be unwise, however, to take current abundance as an indicator of future supply. In fact, the urgency of cocoa sustainability discussions – and remedial actions – has been escalating. While it is difficult to identify the single most pressing threat, climate change is one of the most grievous, not least because it is impacting West Africa particularly harshly. There is an expectation of progressively severe dry seasons in West Africa's growing zone. As El Niño cycles intensify, the region experiences crueler weather, including drought; during these cycles, cocoa production reduces by 2.4 percent on average.[17]

Climate change also exacerbates threats from disease and pests, which have always plagued the fragile *Theobroma cacao* tree. The most widespread disease is black pod, which is present in all major growing regions, though it is most impactful in West Africa. When a tree is infected, pods develop lesions, then turn black and shrivel up. In 2001, researchers estimated that 450,000 MT of cocoa were lost to black pod, which meant over $400 million in lost revenue for farmers.[18] Confined at present to Latin America and the Caribbean, a fungus causes the disease witches' broom, taking energy away from cocoa so that seeds may not develop and ones that do may not be usable. In the early 1900s, Ecuador fell from its position as the world's largest producer when it lost much of its crop to witches' broom. In the late 1900s, the disease destroyed more than a third of Brazil's crop; yields only began to recover in 2014, after enormous effort to combat the disease.[19] A different fungus in Latin America causes frosty pod rot, attacking mainly young pods, which develop a whitish coating that looks like frost. While outbreaks can be destructive, losses have been less than for witches' broom. In West Africa, mealybugs infect trees with swollen shoot virus, causing them to lose leaves, produce lower yields, or die.[20] In Asia, the cocoa pod borer moth lays its eggs on cocoa pods. Larvae bore into the pods, where they feed on pulp and seeds; unchecked, they can cause significant loss.[21]

Growers, agricultural extension officers, and scientists have long sought to control these pests and diseases. Farmers use a variety of methods, including integrated pest management, specific pruning techniques, removing infected tree parts, frequent harvests, applying pesticides, herbicides, and fungicides, and using fertilizers. While each of these can reduce impact, eradication does not seem possible at this point. The method that currently receives the most attention is developing cocoa strains that are genetically resistant to disease. In 2015, James Richardson of the Royal Botanic Garden Edinburgh published the results of research he had conducted with colleagues from Argentina, Colombia, and the US into cocoa's evolutionary history.[22] The group found evidence that the species *cacao* was ten million years old, making it among the oldest of the *Theobroma* genus. The reason why this finding was important to cocoa's sustainability is that when a species is as old as ten million years, it has had time to develop genetic diversity. Cultivated cocoa has low genetic variation, making it even more vulnerable to threats. The news that diverse wild strains might be utilized to improve cocoa's genetic defenses was welcome.

But there remain many perils. The ideal growing

conditions for *Theobroma cacao* are those in which it evolved: under forest cover, protected from direct sunlight and strong wind. Widespread deforestation across cocoa's tropical growing zone means less ideal habitat for sustainable production. Aging trees are declining in productivity, and cocoa monocultures have produced soil fatigue. The increasing cost of inputs adds to farmers' economic difficulties, and there are countless challenges to ensuring that five million growers have access to the most relevant and effective technologies.[23] In the parts of West Africa (including areas of Ghana and Nigeria) where land is divided among siblings at inheritance, farm acreage – and therefore potential cocoa income – has become smaller with each generation, making livelihoods even more precarious. And because young people generally do not want to follow in their parents' footsteps and become cocoa farmers, it is unclear who will maintain the foundation of the industry.[24]

While near-term forecasts are for an increasing world crop, this does not mean every farmer is growing more, healthy cocoa herself or himself. Rather, predicted rises reflect new areas under cultivation and more widespread use of technologies, such as hybrids, that increase yields – but which also deplete the soil and reduce genetic diversity. And while there is room left for expansion, even within West Africa (for example, in January 2017 Nigeria vowed to become the world's largest cocoa exporter),[25] *Theobroma cacao* is already growing in every region that can support it. Cocoa cultivation did shift beyond the Americas on a large scale, but this took decades, if not centuries, and colonialism played a key role (see chapter 2). In the short term, major geographical shifts are not as elastic for cocoa as for other export crops, such as oil palm – not to mention manufactured goods, whose factories move speedily from one country to another as multinationals seek lower costs.

More likely is that a country growing small amounts of cocoa – India, for example – will bring more land under cultivation, as Malaysia and Indonesia did in the 1980s, or that a historical grower – Brazil or Mexico, for example – will revive production significantly. A regional shift to Central Africa, where growers already produce small amounts, is also possible. But each of these scenarios would require impinging upon an environment that is inherently more important than cocoa farmland (such as rainforest), or that many farmers switch to cocoa from whatever they are cultivating for subsistence or sale. It is challenging to imagine the latter, given the long period between planting cocoa trees and earning income, particularly in 2017, when the price is extremely low.

Given these threats, and the fact that even where consumer demand has seemingly plateaued, people still want to eat a lot of chocolate, there are predictions for a supply shortfall. In chapter 8, I examine this anticipated gap in more detail. As with everything about cocoa, references to its sustainability – including quantitative measurements, such as how much cocoa the world can expect to see in years to come – are politicized. In the final chapter, I look at how different actors across the industry shape sustainability discussions, and whose priorities tend to dominate.

Power and politics

As with sustainability, we must look carefully at who or what holds power over people, ideas, practices, and products in cocoa trading. For example, no matter how much cocoa it exports, the government of every producer country holds power over its farmers, who have only rarely exerted collective influence as a voting bloc. But states are subject to other powers. In this book, I look particularly at how colonialism shaped contemporary cocoa geopolitics: first, colonization of the Americas by Spain and Portugal and, later, the scramble for Africa, especially by France and Britain (see chapter 2). More recently – since the 1980s – cocoa exporting states have been subject to neoliberalism: the belief that governments should play as small a role as possible – ideally, none – in the economy or anything else. Rather, market forces (that is, supply and demand) are meant to govern *all* aspects of life, including social welfare. As part of structural adjustment programs (SAPs) in the 1980s and 1990s, neoliberal policies were implemented in every cocoa growing country to their fullest extent, with the exception of Ghana, which resisted certain measures (see chapter 4). While sometimes successful by its own estimation, neoliberalism has typically been to the benefit of a few at the expense of many. Evidence throughout this book challenges the fundamental neoliberal belief that humans are solely motivated by efficient maximization of personal profit, and material from Ghana points to the importance of a strong state role in maintaining production of high-quality cocoa.

Neoliberalism is not the only contested power: farmers, shoppers, governments, non-governmental organizations, and manufacturers can destabilize hierarchies that prevail in the cocoa trade. People do not always act in ways prescribed by social norms of gender, for example, and not every consumer chooses the cheapest bar on the shelf. Though elites benefit at every level of the supply chain, their power is not total. Throughout the cocoa industry, spaces open up – and sometimes are forced open – in which people creatively and vigorously contest dominant structures. If we reject the idea that men, white people, the Netherlands, the Mars family, or Barry Callebaut company were each destined by some natural order to reign over the exchange of a bitter seed, then we can turn our attention to *why* cocoa power has settled into the patterns that it has, and what it will take to change these.

One reason is that cocoa has never been simply a fruit that people liked to turn into a drink or food. From the earliest records of its uses among the Olmec, Maya, and Aztec civilizations, cocoa has always been politicized. In comparison with other food commodities, cocoa has a wide range of values – social, cultural, economic, psychological, physiological, emotional, and so forth – and this book explores many of them. But no matter how else it is valued, cocoa is always a political tool. Every actor in the industry – from nation-states to farmers, from shoppers to manufacturers, and even journalists and researchers – uses cocoa to achieve a goal or benefit, and often this means asserting power. At the producer end, where farmers are selling the fruits of their labor, such moments of power exertion tend to be, if not always highly visible, then at least identifiably political. For example, we can see national politics at work when the postcolonial government of Ghana set a very low producer price for cocoa to fund development projects (see chapter 4).[26] We can see gender politics in the common problem of husbands refusing to share cocoa earnings with their wives and children (see chapters 5 and 6).

The further we move from growing contexts, though, the more challenging it becomes to see the politics of cocoa – yet it remains highly politicized. For example, activists and journalists publicize the issue of child labor on West Africa's cocoa farms, striking a dramatic chord with consumers by telling them enslaved children made their best-loved treat. The regularity of media attention to this issue, especially around Valentine's Day,[27] and the confidence with which reporters, bloggers, and so forth claim frighteningly high rates of child slavery obscure an important fact: that there is a lack of credible information and systematic research into cocoa slavery. Researchers who have investigated child labor have found evidence for lower rates of slavery, and a more complex set of contributing factors, than sensational media accounts suggest; I discuss this research in chapter 6. This is not to say that child slavery is not real – it is. And even if researchers found just one unfree laborer, adult or child, working on a cocoa farm, that would be an abhorrent finding. My goal is not to diminish the issue, but to point out how its representation in Western contexts, and particularly the US, is politicized – and racialized.

For example, the grassroots activist site Slave Free Chocolate, based in California, which describes itself as a "thought leader on this subject,"[28] makes the claim that "Cocoa from outside West Africa is almost always ethically grown."[29] This phrasing implies that the reverse is also true – that cocoa *from* West Africa is almost always *un*ethically grown – making this one of the more blatant anti-Africa statements I have come across in my years of researching the industry. It is also unfounded. Investigations of child labor have focused mainly on Ivory Coast and Ghana,[30] so there is no body of evidence to back up the assertion that the other three million or so cocoa growers around the world all conduct their business ethically. It ignores the history of cocoa slavery in Central and South America and the Caribbean (see chapter 2),[31] as well as contemporary accounts of child labor in those regions. While I caution that any measurements at the global scale are always rough estimates, a 2013 report by the International Programme on the Elimination of Child Labour (IPEC) makes it clear that child labor is a global issue. The report noted that while sub-Saharan Africa has the highest rate of child labor overall (not just in cocoa), that rate declined during the study period (2008–12). During that same period, rates of children undertaking hazardous work were estimated to have *risen* slightly in Latin America and the Caribbean. And while its rate of hazardous child work also declined, Asia Pacific remains the region with the largest absolute number of child laborers.[32] It is irresponsible to make the baseless claim that West Africa is the only "problem" region, all the more so because it appears on the page titled "Ethical Chocolate Companies," to which visitors are likely to navigate when seeking information they can act upon.

Groundless though it is, the claim is probably there because it reduces a complex and under-studied issue to a simple statement that conscientious consumers can remember when they are shopping for chocolate: "West Africa = bad. Everywhere else = good." But the suggestion that all West African cocoa is "bad" also fits neatly with longstanding Western media representations of black Africans as primitive and backward.[33] Such derogatory, debasing representations can make it seem plausible that West Africans today still practice horrors, such as slavery, that the rest of the world has consigned to history – though, as researcher and writer Kevin Bales has amply demonstrated, slavery persists globally, including in the US and Europe.[34] To put it bluntly, the assumption that black Africans enslave their own children in vast numbers is a race-based stereotype. In what may be a challenging notion to accept, buying chocolate made only from cocoa grown "outside" West Africa gains no more than the feeling of guilt-free luxury consumption. Anyone who promotes this story is using cocoa as a political tool to the exclusive benefit of chocolate shoppers – and to themselves if they are getting paid or are otherwise compensated to convey information about chocolate origins. They do this by asserting the power of communicating a false story about West Africans – that they are all evil child abusers – who cannot really assert *their* truth – of being hardworking, honest farmers who love their children – in response. It does not matter that the intention of helping children is a worthy one; cocoa is still politicized to the benefit of a few.

A different example comes from craft chocolate makers, whose numbers have recently multiplied in the US and, at a somewhat slower rate, Europe. These small-batch makers often cite a love of chocolate and desire for hands-on labor with cocoa as motivation for starting what is a risky business endeavor.[35] And for many of them, the work has brought fulfillment, as well as joy to their customers – both worthy accomplishments. But the success of the craft segment is not due only to the skills or tireless labor of these makers. For the most part, they are middle class white men who live in or near urban centers with some foodie presence (that is, potential customers).[36] While this is certainly not the case for every individual among them, on the whole that demographic tends to have privileged access to start-up capital, social capital (a network of helpful connections), learning opportunities, and personal and state-supported safety nets in the event of failure. As men, they are also more likely to have been socialized into learning the mechanical skills needed to operate chocolate-making equipment.

All of those privileges are much less common for people who grow cocoa – not to mention women, people of color, and working class or poor people in North America and Europe. Young people from cocoa producing countries typically find farming a socially undesirable and economically dismal prospect. They too seek more fulfilling labor.[37] But for the entrepreneurs among *them*, the option of starting a high-risk craft chocolate business, using the crop that their families, friends, and neighbors produce, is almost non-existent. As always, there are exceptions. Two self-described pan-African sisters, Priscilla and Kimberly

Addison, opened a craft chocolate company in Ghana in 2016, called '57 Chocolate in reference to Ghana's year of independence from Britain.[38] But we cannot take the success of two young black African women – even if it were to multiply a hundredfold – as proof that becoming a craft chocolate maker is as achievable for everyone in West Africa as it is for white, middle class men in the US or Europe. It is not, and that is a political reality: on the basis of their gender, race, class, and nationality, a limited group of people is able to benefit from cocoa in a way that people who fall differently along those social axes mostly do not.

I myself enjoy a similar advantaged relationship with cocoa. I do not make chocolate, and I am not privileged by my gender or, for much of my life, my class, having grown up in a mostly working class family. However, I have always been privileged by my race and nationality. As a white American, I was able not only to access higher education opportunities to learn about cocoa, but to freely move in and out of farming regions in Asia Pacific and Africa to gain field expertise.[39] My race and national privileges come with social capital, such that even when I first began studying cocoa, I was able to network with managers and gain access to farms. These privileges also afforded me a level of personal health and safety that contrasted starkly with that of the people whose labor I was studying. When I developed appendicitis during my doctoral fieldwork, in a remote location in Ghana, I was able to arrange for immediate transport to a hospital in Accra for surgery, convalesce in the best accommodations on offer, and cover my costs. In a similar situation, the farmers around me would have faced graver circumstances. My knowledge of the cocoa industry is in large part thanks to them but, due to our relative privileges, I went on to return to the US, earn my PhD, secure a faculty position at a respected institution, and earn my living by researching, writing, and teaching about cocoa and chocolate. The farmers, so far as I know, have carried on as they were. Moreover, my success as a scholar is not only because I work hard at my research and at communicating my findings, but also because the thing I study is sexy and alluring. *Cocoa enables me* to research and write in a way that other commodities would not, and has facilitated and expanded my opportunities to earn a living (including writing this book). Thanks to cocoa, I enjoy the work that I do every day. It is a political tool that I use to my benefit.

You may be wondering, after reading these examples, if I believe no one should use cocoa to any personal advantage except impoverished farmers. That is not the case. I chose these examples because they show that no matter how benevolent, laudable, or respectable our intentions may be when it comes to cocoa, no one is free of its politics. Every person who participates in this value chain – including consumers – is in a relative position of power. Everyone can claim some power *over* others (even if they do not exert that power intentionally), and at the same time is *subject to* more powerful people and entities (even if they do not consciously feel the impact of that power). Arguably, this is the case for every commodity chain. But because cocoa is manufactured into a luxury so dear to so many, so accessible as an everyday moment of bliss, it comes with a different kind of emotional power than, say, oil or grains. The implicit call to action here is challenging: it is a request that *everyone* who uses cocoa ask how they personally benefit from it, and how that benefit derives from their relative power. There are many calls for justice in this industry. To succeed, they will require the hard work of interrogating personal privilege when it comes to cocoa.

Another way of thinking about this is that as thoroughly as human beings have politicized cocoa, cocoa has also politicized *us*. Though the first Europeans who encountered cocoa in Mesoamerica didn't think much of it, it was not long before cocoa became prized far afield from its indigenous home. As it spread, cocoa exerted a particular power over people whose cultures had never before known it. Though the introduction of new food crops from the Americas revolutionized diets worldwide, cocoa invited a high degree of political energy and organization, as both tree crop and consumable. It has prompted the formation of international organizations, state regulatory bodies, and non-governmental action groups; it has shifted political economies of agriculture and social relations of gender, ethnicity, class, and age;[40] and it has offered new or intensified modes of personal expression (for example, in its romantic symbolism as chocolate). Few food crops – including others indigenous to the Americas – can match cocoa's ability to harness political will. There is, for example, no International Pumpkin Organization, though pumpkins are culinarily versatile and healthful, are prized far beyond their native home, and have a passionate following and strong holiday ties in the Americas. Vanilla, a close indigenous neighbor of cocoa, is an important agricultural export for countries around the world and a frequent ingredient in chocolate. But there is no flood of newspaper and radio reports on vanilla's origins, price, and labor politics at Valentine's Day. And few advocate for slave-free tomatoes, despite the award-winning journalism of Barry Estabrook, who revealed cases of tomato slave labor in the US state of Florida, where growers of this kitchen staple have been chained and held behind bars at gunpoint.[41]

We *care* about cocoa, to the point of fetishization. From government pronouncements in early 2017 that *it* would soon be the world's largest exporter, we can gather that Nigeria – long among the top five producers – was stung by its recent loss of position to Ecuador. In cocoa's iterations as super-luxury – from Nestlé's production of 24-karat gold KitKat bars in Melbourne,[42] to a Valentine's chocolate cake decorated with 125 diamonds, which retailed for ¥14.1 million (more than $166,000 at the time) in Osaka,[43] to To'ak Chocolate's limited run "vintage" chocolate, cask-aged for eighteen months and priced at $345 for a 50-gram bar[44] – we see the accumulation of centuries of high sociocultural status, manifesting in grotesque price points. In this way, cocoa beans – which have very low use value – start to look like diamonds, whose principal utility is their ability to cut and drill other hard things, but which command incredibly high exchange value when they are of gem quality – because they sparkle.[45]

With these power relationships, market patterns, and hierarchies in mind, we can enter the world of cocoa, but for a brief note on terms. While they have shifting boundaries and no fixed definition, I tend to use "Global South" and "Global North" to make economic distinctions, the former to categorize countries that rely on commodity export, and the latter for industrialized nation-states. When referring to how North American and European media *represent* other parts of the world, I tend to use "Western," as in "Western representations of black African women in advertisements." Debates rage over the use of "cocoa" versus "cacao," and enough ink has been spent for anyone interested to learn more.[46] I use "cocoa" consistently in this book, per both my usual practice and the title suggested by Polity. "Cocoa" is the standard word in Anglophone growing countries, where I have conducted most of my fieldwork, and is the choice of the International Cocoa Organization (ICCO) and World Cocoa Foundation; on futures exchanges, the commodity is traded as cocoa. No doubt my use of it will range from vaguely irritating to heretical among readers habituated to "cacao," especially within the US craft community, which has accorded that word some honor. But hopefully they will find it in their hearts to lay aside the debate. In the end, the beans do not care what we call them. Our concern must be with other politics.

CHAPTER TWO

World Cocoa Map

Ten million years ago, a tree appeared in the northern parts of South America. This was long before *Homo sapiens* arrived, so there was no human witness to the birth of a species that would one day bring taste pleasure to millions. Even if there had been such a witness, she would probably not have guessed that *Theobroma cacao* would become the foundation of an industry that makes $100 billion by selling thin, flat bars. Nothing about the tree suggests a relationship with industrial chocolate. Though I had loved chocolate for all my life, the first time I saw *Theobroma cacao*, in my early thirties, I was startled by its alien strangeness. Its oblong pods were weighty and sculpted, with parallel grooves forming elongated ridges down the length, like so many spines (see figure 2.1). Each one burst forth directly from the trunk and looked invitingly like a weapon: an aerodynamic projectile whose heft could certainly dent a soft target. But they were also beautiful. Soft olive-mint, lemon yellow, or a deep red somewhere between wine and crimson, the pods seemed like objects that a giant would string together to wear as a necklace.

To produce such alluring fruit, *Theobroma cacao* requires a specific set of environmental conditions. The shape and chemistry of its flowers attract almost exclusively midges – tiny flies – and, in their absence, pollination is less likely to occur. European settlers arriving in the Americas learned this when they attempted to "clean up" indigenous farms.

Figure 2.1 Ripening cocoa pods, Aduyaakrom, Ghana © Kristy Leissle

Once they had cleared out decaying leaves and arranged the trees in rows, the midges – which prefer a messy environment – flew away and the trees bore no fruit. Even when it does produce pods, *Theobroma cacao* cannot propagate without help.[1] While we refer to cocoa "beans," they are *not* legumes. Legume pods can open naturally as they mature; for example, a peapod splits along its seam. Cocoa pods, in contrast, are thick and sturdy, and they do not fall from the tree and break apart on their own. Squirrels, bats, and monkeys will dig through the pod to get at the sticky fruit inside, leaving the bitter seeds behind. Humans eventually did the same.

Cocoa's development into industrial chocolate was perhaps an unlikely destiny. For Europeans first encountering cocoa, knowledge of temperate fruits – apples, for example – gave little botanical guidance, though they may have found it easier to comprehend the fact that cocoa had religious significance. In the Judeo-Christian tradition, the apple, representing knowledge, plays a central role in the origin story of Adam and Eve: it was the temptation that led to their downfall. In Mesoamerica, cocoa's religious significance was positive and the fruit was revered. In Maya and Aztec cultures, the gods provided recipes for making cocoa drinks, which gave those drinks high status and political significance. This religious history prompted Swedish botanist Carl Linnaeus to assign the tree's genus the name *Theobroma*, which translates as "food of the gods." In most other ways, however, apples and cocoa are very much unalike. An apple dangles on a thin stem from the outer branches of a deciduous tree, *Malus domestica*. Thin, slightly waxy skin encases mature fruit, and human teeth can easily puncture this skin to get to the prize: plump, solid flesh. This contains fiber and vitamins, but our attraction is to the sugars: fructose, sucrose, and glucose. Buried in apple flesh are tiny seeds, which, when chewed and digested, release cyanide. While the risk of being poisoned is low, humans tend to avoid them. In contrast, a cocoa pod is impenetrable without a sharp tool, such as a machete, or prolonged gnawing. The fruit inside is not solid, but a sticky whitish pulp called mucilage. Like apple flesh, cocoa pulp contains sugars but, as a pasty substance, it's hard to take a bite out of it. Forest animals will lick pulp off the seeds, and it was almost certainly pulp that initially attracted people to *Theobroma cacao*. There is evidence that in their earliest uses of the fruit, people in Central and South America consumed raw pulp, made fermented drinks from it, and used it medicinally, even as an aid to childbirth.[2] Nowadays, farmers consume pulp as refreshment in a humid, hot growing environment. However, the pulp is not the main attraction of the cocoa pod today. Instead, we use the seeds.

Fresh from the pod, the seed can be bitter and nauseating to eat, even in small quantities. For its early users, this bitterness may have suggested the seeds had medicinal properties, a possibility that remains attractive to chocolate lovers today. Contrary to popular belief, cocoa is not high enough in caffeine content to have much effect on the human central nervous system. However, it does contain higher concentrations of a related (though weaker) alkaloid, theobromine, which can have a stimulant effect on heart rate and lessen coughs. It may be that once people discovered these or other properties, they looked for ways to transform raw cocoa into something more palatable. Today, the first steps in this transformation are fermentation and drying. Whoever initially applied these techniques to cocoa lived long before any historical record, so we can only make educated guesses about why they did so. Humans may have first learned to ferment and roast other foods, and then tried these out on cocoa. Researchers are also unclear how *Theobroma cacao* cultivation moved within and between Central and South America. It is possible that the tree spread naturally, but it is also likely that people moved it, exchanging processing techniques and developing new ones as they went.[3] What we do know is that when Europeans encountered cocoa as part of Spanish and Portuguese colonization of the Americas, the world cocoa map began a dramatic shift that has persisted to this day.

Cocoa's indigenous map

There is evidence for much earlier use, but most historical accounts of *Theobroma cacao* begin with the Olmecs, a civilization that predominated in present-day Mexico, on the Gulf coast, and whose influence extended as far south as Honduras or Nicaragua, from around 1400 to 400 BCE.[4] Perhaps having learned from their predecessors, the Olmecs made drinks out of cocoa seeds; the Olmecs then influenced Maya and Aztec civilizations in their uses of the fruit. Culturally, from at least 1000 BCE, people from present-day Mexico through Costa Rica have held cocoa in high regard. Its uses in pre-conquest Mesoamerica – that is, before Hernando Cortez and his forces conquered the Aztecs, in 1521 – fell into three main categories: as drink, cultural symbol, and currency.

Though people across socioeconomic groups in Mesoamerica consumed cocoa, historians and archaeologists have uncovered the most evidence for its status as a drink of the Maya and Aztec elite, especially nobility and wealthy merchants; warriors also drank it. It is possible that these groups left more records, though, so we may never know the extent of cocoa's use among commoners. There is, however, abundant evidence that cocoa in all its forms was a political tool, and played a role in negotiations and power displays. For example, feasts among the Maya political and economic elite involved cocoa for lavish food presentations and gift exchanges. These feasts celebrated significant political events, such as royal marriage or military victory; in that context, serving cocoa was a way to display wealth, and therefore power.[5] Rituals of drinking and eating together were also part of the process by which Maya elites finalized political pacts and commercial affairs, such as selling cocoa farmland.[6] As regional currency, cocoa had a public role in politics: conquered peoples throughout Mesoamerica paid rulers tribute in beans, a form of wealth extraction by the powerful from the weak.[7]

Unlike today, women and children seem to have had less access to cocoa than adult men, although there is evidence that women were responsible for making the drinks.[8] Historical evidence describes many preparation methods, which produced drinks of varying thickness (often using ground maize), color, and temperature. Sometimes, flavorings were added, including vanilla, honey, and chilies. A feature largely lost today was a prized foam, created by pouring cocoa liquid from one vessel to another from a height. Because recipes originated with the gods, cocoa drinks were considered to have powerful physiological effects. The most precious recipes promised virility, strength, and the fortitude to undertake physically demanding feats, such as marching to war. All this meant that among Aztec and Maya people, cocoa drinks were highly masculinized – a remarkable difference to contemporary associations of chocolate with women.

Today, we use cocoa seeds to make chocolate and skincare products; in pre-conquest Mesoamerica, their role extended to rituals. Ceremonies for coming of age, holidays, and ritual sacrifice involved cocoa. Far from romance and frosted cupcakes, anthropologist Cameron McNeil notes strong ties between cocoa and death in ancient Mesoamerica. For example, in present-day Honduras, there is archaeological evidence of cocoa trees depicted with the faces of dead ancestors, reborn as *Theobroma cacao*. Whereas today, "shade-grown" labels are sometimes used on chocolate bars to suggest environmentally beneficial growing conditions, in pre-conquest times, cocoa's "ties to the shade . . . encouraged its association with death and the Underworld."[9] Use of the achiote plant to color cocoa drinks red has been linked to blood symbolism, and pods were depicted as bleeding in the same way as a human heart – or as being blessed with self-sacrificed blood from the gods.[10] Histories of cocoa in Mesoamerica sometimes reference its role in rituals of human sacrifice, especially among the Aztecs.[11] A great deal of controversy surrounds accounts of sacrifice, not least because Spanish chroniclers likely exaggerated the number of victims to depict the Aztecs as barbaric, and thus "rationalize" their own country's conquest methods – which, by any account, killed far more people. I raise the subject to emphasize cocoa's political force in rituals. Mesoamericans made sacrifices, of humans or otherwise, to ensure stability or prosperity for the living. Sacrifices were an offer of something valuable to secure a boon from a more powerful entity. Particularly as a metaphor for blood, cocoa was an esteemed addition to these offerings.

Cocoa's non-food uses were not, however, exclusively morbid. By at least 400 BCE, the beans served as trading currency across Mesoamerica, and there is evidence that they made it as far north as present-day New Mexico in the US.[12] Laborers were paid with cocoa and traders made counterfeit cocoa currency. While its role as money declined post-conquest, transactions using cocoa have been documented through 1750 in Mexico City, and as recently as the 1840s in the Yucatan peninsula.[13] Cocoa's use as currency was tied to its social significance. For example, Maya royalty were sometimes buried with beans to send them into the next world with financial security – and luxurious drinks. Since *Theobroma cacao* did not thrive everywhere in Mesoamerica, certain areas grew more money than others, including parts of present-day Guatemala, El Salvador, and Nicaragua. When the Aztecs rose to prominence, the seat of empire, Tenochtitlan (today's Mexico City), was not an area that could produce cocoa. So, the Aztec ruler received beans as tribute from places that could, no matter how far distant, and regardless of the long overland journeys required to deliver the wealth.[14]

Commodification intensifies

The first Europeans to lay eyes on cocoa did not recognize its economic, social, or cultural value. In 1502, when he met indigenous people ferrying beans in canoes off the coast of Honduras, Christopher Columbus's son Ferdinand called them "almonds" and wondered at the great care Amerindians took with them.[15] Though Columbus sent some back to his patrons in Spain, King Ferdinand and Queen Isabella, neither the explorer, his son, nor those rulers understood their importance. It was not until Hernando Cortez arrived with his conquistadores, landing among the Aztecs in 1518 and in control by 1521, that Europeans began to appreciate cocoa. Writing in the mid-sixteenth century, chroniclers tell us that a small rabbit was worth 10 to 30 beans and a (presumably meatier) "forest" rabbit cost 100. You could buy a horse or mule for 50, and a piece of cloth for 80 to 100; a slave also cost 100. Beans themselves had different values. A "good turkey hen" was worth "100 full cacao beans, or 120 shrunken cacao beans."[16]

It is even more illuminating to comprehend cocoa's value in pre-conquest Mesoamerica through its *socioeconomics*. The prestige of cocoa drinks gave them a role in maintaining Maya and Aztec gender norms and class hierarchies. For example, that subjugated people paid tribute in beans and that women and commoners were responsible for making cocoa drinks suggest that cocoa *production* was linked to low socioeconomic status. Its *consumption*, however, most often indicated high status. When Europeans arrived, cocoa continued to reflect these social hierarchies. However, European colonization of the Americas brought intensified forms of subjugation. Cocoa's production and consumption began to both shape and reflect a new *global* socioeconomic stratification. For example, just as the Aztec ruler had forced subjects to pay tribute in cocoa beans, so too did Cortez. Colonists arriving from Spain (at least, those well connected to imperial rulers) were granted the right to exact cocoa tribute from indigenous farmers, which included forced labor. While paying tribute in cocoa was not new, and continued to reflect growers' subjection to oppressive rulers, the supply chain – that is, where beans went after they left the farm – shifted dramatically.

Cocoa no longer remained in Mesoamerican circulation, but instead was shipped to Europe. There, a group of elite people who had never seen or heard of it before began to drive its trade. While production–consumption patterns had always reflected economic divisions and gender- and class-based hierarchies, now its trade supplanted cocoa's Mesoamerican sociocultural embeddedness, and cocoa took the first steps toward becoming a global commodity. This shift destabilized and, in some cases, severed cocoa's links to its Mesoamerican roots. For farmers who adopted the crop in Africa and Asia Pacific, cocoa had no social meaning. It was a raw material, grown for export, whose final form and value farmers scarcely comprehended. After a while, for consumers, cocoa's distinction as finished luxury bore little, if any, relationship to origins.

The trading map shifted to encompass two distinct goods: cocoa and chocolate. For all its history prior to European colonization, cocoa as fruit on a tree, as currency, and as drink had been deeply connected, within civilizational traditions that barely distinguished between its economic, social, cultural, and food values. Now, those values diverged. Far from its roots as a gods-given boon, cocoa's sociocultural value in Europe and, eventually, North America diminished. As far as its new traders were concerned, cocoa was fungible, each bean just as tradable as the next, with no particular meaning attached. Meanwhile, industrial bar chocolate – unknown in Mesoamerica – ultimately acquired sociocultural value to the point of fetishization.

This change did not happen overnight. Official (that is, taxed) shipments of beans began to arrive in Europe in the late 1500s, a century after Columbus first saw them. A few decades later, cocoa drinks started to gain popularity in elite European enclaves. As Cortez and his conquistadores, mingling with the Aztecs, developed a taste for cocoa, they sent drinks recipes back to Europe, as did the missionaries and merchants who played a lively role in extending cocoa's popularity beyond its indigenous home. At first, the only people in Europe who drank cocoa were Spanish royalty and their courts. Thanks to intermarriages between royal families and the circulation of fashionable trends among them, a taste for the drinks spread, first to southern Europe, then northward. As people began to drink cocoa in Europe's predominantly Catholic south, its consumption was politicized – thanks to the question of whether drinking it constituted a violation of pre-Communion or Lenten fasts.[17] Christians in Chiapas had put the question in 1577 to Pope Gregory XIII, who said that cocoa did not break the fast. Subsequent popes concurred but, without an official papal bull, the matter remained contentious. As Marcy Norton has documented, some of the leading Spanish intellectuals, religious figures, and physicians debated the issue throughout the early 1600s, as did everyday people.[18] It was a question of political significance. Having begun in 1517, the Protestant Reformation was still challenging the legitimacy of Catholic doctrine, and alleging corruption among church leadership. Debates over cocoa's "food" status were part of a paradigm-shifting interrogation of the religious canon and political power of the Roman Catholic Church that spanned more than a century.

Thus politicized, cocoa made its way through Western Europe. During the 1600s, people beyond the aristocracy started to enjoy the drink, especially in Britain. Coffee, cocoa, and tea were all new to Britain in the early seventeenth century. As historian Matthew Green has documented, while cocoa remained by and large an elite drink in continental Europe, in Britain, a new class of "intelligentsia," as we might call them today, adopted the drink.[19] These men spent time in London's new coffee and chocolate houses, talking politics. Thus, in their early British social life, cocoa drinks retained historical Mesoamerican machismo: drinking cocoa in seventeenth-century London happened in highly masculinized, politicized spaces. Though unseemly at times, chocolate houses gave cocoa drinks a social foothold beyond the aristocracy. It would take another century or so before the Industrial Revolution brought cocoa products into widespread consumption, but the process had begun.

Production shifts

As men debated politics over cocoa drinks in London, its growers in Mesoamerica were suffering. The sustained violence of colonization and spread of previously unknown European diseases had devastated indigenous populations, as well as their farms. But colonizers now wanted to drink cocoa too, as did their compatriots in Europe. Cocoa plantings began to spread beyond Mesoamerica, and the tree's travels were a microcosm of changes sweeping the world at the time. The post-conquest world was one of intense globalization, as colonists, merchants, missionaries, and pirates moved novel goods and ideas between the New and Old Worlds and beyond. Economic historian William Gervase Clarence-Smith has traced the spread of cocoa from the seventeenth through nineteenth centuries, from exogenous plantings that began across the Caribbean, to sub-Saharan Africa and Asia.[20] Cocoa traveled from Venezuela around Africa to Sri Lanka, and from Central America westward, to the Philippines. A century later, widespread cultivation had spread to the Bahia region of Brazil, and cocoa went from Sri Lanka through the Asia Pacific islands, including Indonesia. In the 1800s, it moved across West, Central, and East Africa, as far as Madagascar, and to Papua New Guinea and India. By the late nineteenth century, cocoa was as global as it ever would be.

With *Theobroma cacao* introduced to virtually every location within the tropical band that could support it, Mesoamerica lost its producer dominance. As Clarence-Smith has documented, for a time, European colonizers used indigenous slaves to grow cocoa.[21] But violence and disease so decimated the indigenous population that, by the mid-1600s, there were not enough people left to enslave. Europeans were able to use temporarily forced labor among the remaining Amerindians (as opposed to enslaving them for life); however, they mostly turned to imported African slaves. Cocoa production shifted from Central to South America, especially Venezuela and Ecuador. Of the two, Venezuela relied more heavily on slave labor. Because it was easier and cheaper to transport slaves from Africa to the Caribbean and Atlantic coastal regions of South America, compared to the Pacific side, cocoa slavery was more common in the former. Free laborers also worked on cocoa farms in Venezuela and the Caribbean, but slaves were frequently the mainstay, and Clarence-Smith notes that cocoa bondage peaked from the 1760s to the 1790s. In contrast, it was more difficult and expensive to access slave labor for cocoa farms in Guayaquil, Ecuador – at the time the second largest producer.[22] Portugal's colony of Brazil later became a major supplier to Europe, as did Spain's Caribbean colony of Trinidad and Tobago; both relied heavily on African slave labor on cocoa and other plantations.

Cruel and exploitative production stood in sharp contrast to the new sociocultural value that cocoa consumables were gaining in Europe. At first, as in Mesoamerica, the drink was gritty and often bitter, its fat difficult to digest. But starting in the 1700s and accelerating in the 1800s, the Industrial Revolution offered new possibilities for enjoying cocoa. Manufacturing innovations began largely in Britain and extended from there to continental Europe and North America. The revolution encompassed a shift from local economies of production – household- or community-based labor systems, where people knew who made the tools they used and the foods they ate – to the anonymous workspace of the factory floor. In factories, machines and new technologies for powering them transformed cocoa products. What had been a thick, expensive drink of the elite became a solid, sweet, smooth, cheap chocolate bar.

The nascent advertising industry gave this novel food an identity. Because so many people across Europe were illiterate, marketing (as it came to be known) relied on images to convey ideas about chocolate. Depictions of upper class people consuming chocolate gave it socioeconomic status,[23] while pictures of cherubs and children invited notions of innocence.[24] Images of people in good health convinced shoppers that chocolate was pure and safe to eat. This last was not simply an advertising invention, but a response to the adulteration of chocolate that was prevalent during the industrializing 1800s. As manufacturers turned out chocolate products, they sought ways to keep production as cheap as possible, including adding unsavory fillers. Sophie D. Coe and Michael D. Coe note the frequent use of potato starch, as well as rice, lentil, or dried pea powder, and even brick dust, to bulk out chocolate. Because cocoa butter was an expensive component, some manufacturers substituted animal fats, including from veal and mutton. Among the accused, Cadbury responded with advertisements promoting its chocolate's purity, which helped the company surpass its competitors.[25] As with Cadbury, the companies pioneering such advertisements became by degrees more successful. At the same time, manufacturers in Britain, Switzerland, and the Netherlands improved existing technologies and introduced innovations, especially the conche by Switzerland's Rodolphe Lindt in 1879, and the Dutching process by Coenraad van Houten in 1828 in the Netherlands. With smoother, creamier, sweeter products rolling out of factories, demand – especially for milk chocolate – rose quickly.

Cocoa imports had already surged ninefold between 1870 and 1900, and rising chocolate demand pushed production to escalate again in the first half of the twentieth century, this time almost fourteenfold: from 53,000 MT in 1900 to 736,000 MT by 1950.[26] This was far more than South American and Caribbean producers alone could provide, especially as witches' broom had by then wiped out much of Ecuador's crop. Too, slavery had been abolished throughout these regions – in 1834 in Trinidad (by then a British colony), 1851 in Ecuador, 1854 in Venezuela, and 1888 in Brazil – cutting off or diminishing one exploitative labor route to high production. Moreover, South American colonies had long since gained independence – Spain lost Ecuador in 1822 and Venezuela in 1819, while Portugal decolonized Brazil in 1822. While this did not immediately transform economic relations between former colonizers and colonies, it did erode the direct political force that Spain and Portugal could use to compel cocoa production.

But two other empire-builders were on the rise in Europe.

Already in possession of colonies and outposts, especially in the Americas and Asia, Britain and France began to build truly global empires. They focused their efforts on Africa. From the late 1800s to the early 1900s occurred what is called the "scramble for Africa," in which nearly the entire continent (about 90 percent) became a colony of Britain, France, or another European power (including Portugal, Belgium, Germany, and Italy). Imperialism was a way for European countries to battle for supremacy, as they took control over territories and populations beyond their borders; they often traded colonies as the spoils of Europe-based wars. It also enabled newly industrializing countries to feed their factories with inputs they could not or did not wish to produce. As Britain and France colonized Africa, they discovered that cocoa flourished in West Africa's tropical forests.

By this time, West African farmers were already cultivating cocoa. Merchants, colonizers, and other travelers had brought seedlings first to Africa's islands. While dates differ depending on source, there is documentation that cocoa had arrived in the Portuguese colonies of São Tomé and Príncipe in the Gulf of Guinea by 1822, and nearby Fernando Po (present-day Bioko, former colony of Spain) by 1836. From these islands, cocoa spread to mainland Africa. It was introduced to Cameroon by 1858, Nigeria by 1874, Ghana by 1876 (its arrival commonly, almost mythically, attributed to a farmer, Tetteh Quarshie, who returned with cocoa from Fernando Po), and Ivory Coast by 1890.

From that point, West Africa saw a phenomenal rise in cocoa production, and the story of how this happened takes several turns. The first important regional producers were São Tomé and Príncipe, tiny islands that supplied nearly a third of the world's cocoa in 1900;[27] that same year, Cadbury purchased almost half its cocoa from São Tomé.[28] Slave labor made such tremendous output possible. Portuguese colonizers imported slaves from their country's territory in Angola and put them to work on plantations a continent away. Though officially they were *serviçais*, or paid laborers who had the right to return home after five years, virtually none did; in every aspect, they were de facto slaves. With journalists reporting on the issue, activists in Britain protested slave production of cocoa. Though it took the better part of a decade, these protests eventually resulted in a Cadbury boycott of São Tomé cocoa in 1909.[29] While São Tomé's role as cocoa exporter declined afterwards, the boycott did not end labor abuses. Clarence-Smith documents the continued use of coerced labor, in São Tomé, Príncipe, and elsewhere in the Gulf of Guinea region for long afterwards.[30]

Cocoa cultivation then shifted to mainland West Africa. Britain looked to the "free" labor, at least compared to slaves elsewhere, of its recently acquired Gold Coast colony (present-day Ghana). Between Britain's Gold Coast and Nigeria, and France's Ivory Coast and Cameroon, West Africa swiftly took command of global production. From this point, Central and South America never regained regional export prominence over what was once their exclusive crop (though individual countries remain significant producers). Keen to meet rising chocolate demand back home, British and French colonial officials adopted various methods to escalate production. Among these was brute force, including the *méthode forte* practiced by French colonizers, which involved physical punishment for not meeting quotas, burning fields, and other cruel acts. Another was the establishment of a taxation system. Though West African merchants had long used currencies across regional trade routes, colonial taxes necessitated greater cash flow. One way to earn more cash was to switch from growing subsistence foods and bartering for necessities, to farming export crops. To meet new tax requirements (such as the head tax France introduced to Ivory Coast in 1900, among many others across the region), farmers faced little choice but to cultivate cash-earning exports. Gold Coast farmers opted for cocoa; Ivory Coast growers initially cultivated more cotton and coffee but, eventually, made a major transition to cocoa too. West African agriculture underwent a profound shift that shapes the region's political economy to this day: from growing food to eat, to growing export crops to sell.

However, colonial pressure was not solely responsible for West Africa's rise. Starting with Polly Hill's research among Gold Coast farmers in the 1950s,[31] scholars have documented farmers' enthusiasm for cocoa. Around the turn of the twentieth century, coffee's price was low and the market for natural rubber was beginning a precipitous decline. In contrast, Europe's seemingly insatiable demand for chocolate assured a steady market for cocoa – whose price had been rising. In the Gold Coast, the constant arrival of migrant laborers from northern regions, eager to farm, meant that available land was soon put to use as a cocoa farm. Combined, these factors made for explosive cocoa growth. Having only started exporting cocoa in the late nineteenth century, in just two decades the Gold Coast became the world's largest supplier, a position it held for most of the twentieth century.

In the 1960s, newly independent Ivory Coast began welcoming migrants to encourage cultivation of cocoa and other crops (see chapter 5). In what became known as the Ivorian miracle, the country experienced remarkable economic growth from expanded export crop production. By the late 1970s, Ivory Coast had surpassed its neighbor

Table 2.1 Top cocoa producers, 2016–2017 season forecast	
Country	World production share (%)
Ivory Coast	41.7
Ghana	18.7
Indonesia	7.2
Ecuador	5.9
Cameroon	5.5
Nigeria	5.1
Brazil	4.2
Peru	2.3
Dominican Republic	1.8
Colombia	1.2
Total for top ten	93.6

Source: QBCS, XLIII, table 4.

– now called Ghana, post-independence – to become the world's largest cocoa exporter (see table 2.1).

More recently, Southeast Asian countries increased production; Indonesia and Malaysia particularly encouraged the crop. Indonesia vastly expanded cultivation in the 1980s, especially on Sulawesi island, to become the third largest producer. As in West Africa, smallholders account for nearly all production; unlike in West Africa, Indonesian growers sell mainly unfermented beans. Malaysia had a different story. With state support, Malaysian growers produced a terrific rise in cocoa volumes in the 1970s and 1980s, and the country became one of the top ten producers. But the position was short-lived. After achieving its highest-ever cocoa output in 1990, Malaysia (along with Indonesia) scaled up cultivation of oil palm. Cocoa exports, which had risen so dramatically in the 1980s, fell with equal drama: by 2013, Malaysia's growers were producing only negligible amounts.[32] Today, the country processes cocoa beans instead of growing them, mostly Indonesian imports.

Though West Africa has long been the world's major growing region, as the Malaysia example illustrates, national positions do shift. Dominican Republic, Peru, and especially Ecuador have been rebuilding export volumes of cocoa beans and products. Battling witches' broom, Brazil was a net importer of cocoa and cocoa products for half the seasons between 2006 and 2014. In the 2014–15 season, however, it became a net exporter again, and ranks among the top ten producers.[33] Venezuela grows prized cocoa, but is struggling to export it due to political instability and violence. In 2014–15, for example, Venezuelan growers produced 16,000 MT of beans, but the country exported just 6,000 MT of cocoa and cocoa products (though domestic demand would account for some, or even much, of the difference).[34] Papua New Guinea is reviving its once-vibrant cocoa sector; if it achieves the ICCO's forecast for 2016–17, of 41,300 MT, it will remain the world's eleventh largest producer.[35] Hawaii – the only place in the US where cocoa grows – is making an innovative contribution, as small-scale manufacturers condense the commodity chain by making chocolate from local beans. While West Africa will likely continue to dominate, there is dynamism throughout cocoa's growing zones.

This world cocoa map needs one final feature: the divide between people who grow cocoa and people who eat industrial bar chocolate. Though they grow more of the crop than anyone else in the world, farmers across West Africa rarely have the opportunity to consume chocolate, apart from weak and sugary cocoa drink mixes. When I am conducting fieldwork in Ghana, though literally surrounded by cocoa, I eat the least chocolate compared to any other time. What little I can find is expensive, often far beyond its shelf life, and typically imported from Southeast Asia. But even when I am in that part of the world, I am able to afford chocolate if I want to buy it. Most farmers there cannot. From my surveys of household food expenditures, a farming family in Ghana's Western region would have to save all the cash normally spent on food over two and a half days to afford one 200-gram Cadbury bar.

I need to contextualize this finding, because chocolate's scarcity does not necessarily deprive Ghanaian farmers of a food they *want* to eat. As I investigated chocolate's availability in Ghana, I also studied food culture. I learned that farmers categorize foods into two types: hard and soft. Hard foods, such as fufu – a starchy meal base made by boiling and pounding plantains, yams, cocoyams, or cassava – provide energy to undertake hard work, including weeding and pruning cocoa farms. Simon Opoku, who worked as a farmer and buyer near to Enchi in the Western region, explained, "If you're taking tea and you go to farm, you will not last. If you go to farm, you take hard food like plantain, cocoyam, yam, so it will last for some hours before you go in." Soft foods – including chocolate – cannot satisfy the energy demands of hard work, and are suitable only for time spent at home or social gatherings, or for people with office jobs. Because Nestlé's Milo drink mix was widely available, growers often referred to Milo in our discussions of chocolate. Simon added, "You can't drink Milo and then go and work hard. You will feel hungry. You cannot work more." We can contrast this with advertising campaigns in mature markets that emphasize chocolate as an energy food – notably Snickers, which Mars has long branded with the idea of hunger satisfaction.[36]

While growers in Ghana may not want to eat chocolate regularly, many expressed the desire for chocolate to be available, as a sign of Ghana's participation in value addition. Chocolate's inaccessibility was a reminder that, though they fed the industry with its most necessary input, farmers remain marginalized from the realm of the finished product. Chapter 3 examines why this is so, starting with the many steps that it takes to turn cocoa beans into chocolate bars.

CHAPTER THREE

Stages of Sweet

Cocoa beans are not very edible, which means they have low use value. Farmers grow them for their exchange value: that is, because they can trade the beans for money. Ebenezer Tandoh, a farmer from Kramokrom in Ghana's Western region, emphasized that as farmers, "We don't have any means of using the commodity or the beans on our own." He had no choice but to sell cocoa from his seven-acre farm, and depended upon those sales to support himself, his wife, and the child they were expecting when we met. This chapter addresses historical and contemporary factors that can help us understand why major cocoa exporting countries – and farmers within them – have been alienated from processes that turn cocoa beans into chocolate bars, and some of the impacts of this disconnect. Especially in West Africa, farmers often undertake the fermentation and drying that begin to transform cocoa into chocolate. But from that point, making chocolate is a manufacturing endeavor that requires substantial capital investment, far beyond the means of most farmers or, until recently, even the largest exporting countries.

This is now changing, and later in this chapter I illustrate how and where processing capacity is expanding. We cannot discount the geopolitical importance of cocoa exporters assuming a greater role in value addition. But nor can we be too cautious in heralding rising value-added exports as an achievement for growers. As I discuss in the conclusion of this chapter, farmers remain disconnected from most material and economic benefits of value addition. Indeed, there is no structural aspect of the industry at present that suggests growers *could* benefit from it. This fact is not lost on farmers in Ghana, and I include some of their comments regarding what they perceive as a rigid and racialized global pattern of industrialization and access to manufactured luxury goods, including chocolate.

To grapple with these cocoa politics, we must first understand how cocoa becomes chocolate. In contrast to dried coffee beans, which need only roasting and grinding to use as the basis for a drink, making chocolate requires many processing steps. In typical order, these are: clean, roast, crack and winnow, mill, mix, refine, conche, temper, mold, cool, and package. And that's just for a chocolate bar. Confectionery (for example, filled truffles and bonbons) requires further steps. A close look at the industrial value chain illustrates its complexity and capital-intensive nature.

Walk through a chocolate factory

Chocolate factories are not all the same. Depending on available capital and wherewithal to acquire machinery, makers may leave out or combine certain steps. Some companies alter or eliminate processes to achieve a particular texture or flavor. Craft makers may do some processing by hand. But to illustrate the full industrial complexity of turning cocoa into chocolate, our imaginary factory will have all the steps.[1]

Because cocoa is often fermented and dried on the ground (for example, in a forest or on the side of a road), it tends to accumulate dirt and (sometimes unusual) debris. Thus beans first enter a cleaning machine, which may use air, gravity, vibration, magnets, and/or sieves to remove unwanted material. Along with stones, wood, leaves, and soil, cleaning machines have unearthed everything from plastic doll parts to bullets. Once these items are removed, the beans go into a roaster, where high temperatures kill any microbes. In addition to sterilizing them, roasting dries the beans further, from about 6 or 8 percent to about 2 percent moisture content. Sometimes, beans are roasted whole to sterilize and dry them, and then again later for flavor development.

Chocolate's flavor, in the words of US craft maker Steve DeVries, develops from "the heat and oxygen that the chocolate 'sees' during its manufacture," from fermentation through tempering.[2] However, roasting is one of the most noticeable moments of flavor change. Roasting machines rotate and tumble cocoa beans over a heat source, at a specific temperature and for a specific duration. Major manufacturers typically roast beans to suit brand recipes; in these cases, makers are looking for flavor consistency. Other makers choose to bring out diverse flavors that naturally occur in cocoa beans (see chapter 7). Moreover, just as some coffee drinkers prefer a light, medium, or dark roast, chocolate makers (or their customers) may prefer a certain roast profile. American craft makers tend toward lighter roasts, which retain fresh, "green" flavors in the chocolate (Dandelion Chocolate[3] bars are a great example), whereas chocolate by French makers often displays characteristics of a dark roast, including notes of wood smoke or toast (bars from François Pralus[4] and Jacques Torres[5] are good illustrations).

From the roaster, beans move to a stage called cracking (or breaking) and winnowing. The cocoa seed has three parts: husk, nib (also called cotyledon), and radical. The husk is a thin outer shell surrounding the seed; during roasting, this papery covering separates a little from the inner nib and becomes easier to remove. Prior to the Industrial Revolution, cocoa beans had to be broken and winnowed by hand. Among the Aztec and Maya civilizations, not all recipes required this step, but many did. Removing husks is a laborious and painful process, as their sharp edges can stab beneath fingernails, and it would have been a grueling task for the women and common laborers who prepared cocoa drinks. Today, a machine usually cracks the beans, loosening or removing parts of the shell and breaking the seed into smaller pieces, which are then called nibs. A winnower sorts nibs into piles of similar size, most often by vibrating them through screens with varying mesh. The winnower may use a magnet to remove metals the cleaner did not catch, and may remove the seed's radical: a tiny particle that looks like a short length of pin. Were the seed to grow into a tree, the radical would become its taproot (central root). It is *extremely* hard; while some makers believe its removal is best for chocolate consistency, most modern machines leave the radical in.

Cracked nibs then go into a mill. There are various mill types, used separately or in combination, including stone, disc, hammer (impact), and ball mills. Their purpose is to grind nibs to a very small size, usually around 30 microns, or 30 millionths of a meter. Reduced to this size, the nibs approach liquid form. The slight increase in temperature that occurs in the mill helps by melting cocoa's naturally occurring fat. The result is a paste-like substance called liquor, though it has no alcohol content. Liquor typically goes next into a mixing machine. For dark chocolate, the mixer will blend in sugar and, for milk chocolate, sugar and milk powder. For either type, a maker may choose to add vanilla as a flavor enhancer.

Because sugar crystals and milk powder are relatively large compared to the milled cocoa particles, the whole mixture goes into a refiner. One of chocolate's attractions is its smooth texture; this is largely determined by the size of the solid particles suspended in the chocolate. Makers achieve ideal size by putting the liquor through two- or five-roll refiners: stacks of cylindrical rollers, moving in opposite directions, with a miniscule space between them. A roll refiner smashes all particles down to around 20 microns, and the mixture comes out the other side as warm, dry (delicious) flake. Refining can be one of the most challenging steps. If particles are too large, we experience the chocolate as having a rough texture. However, if particles are too small, we will also experience that as a negative sensation, which some connoisseurs call "dirt mouth." For me, this feels as if the chocolate is vacuuming all the saliva from my mouth. DeVries explains that this happens when "too-small particles get stuck in the taste buds and do not clear the mouth, leaving a clay-ey texture."[6]

By this stage, we can call the mixture chocolate, but several steps remain before the finished bar. Most factories move the chocolate next to a conche, a machine that Swiss maker Rodolphe Lindt invented in 1879. Some makers, particularly large volume manufacturers, may add lecithin at this stage. Most commercial lecithin is derived from soy, and soy lecithin's job is to control the viscosity of molten chocolate. Viscosity is the potential of a material to flow: the higher its viscosity, the more resistant chocolate is to flowing; at a lower viscosity, chocolate is more fluid. To make chocolate flow well for the rest of processing and to give it a desirable texture, one option is to add more cocoa butter. However, cocoa butter is expensive – in fact, the most expensive semi-finished product made from cocoa beans. Large manufacturers often opt for lecithin as a cheaper alternative. Colin Gasko, craft chocolate maker, explains that "lecithin, when added in amounts below 1 percent, drastically reduces the viscosity of chocolate, much more than cocoa butter would. Lecithin, being a cheap byproduct of soybean oil refining, is a simple way of cost saving in chocolate where cocoa butter is the most expensive component."[7]

Whether to add lecithin is just one choice a manufacturer must make at the conching stage, which is another moment of noticeable flavor development.[8] A conche is a vat in which paddles, blades, or rollers continually move molten chocolate, for periods from several hours to several days. The resulting heat and shearing action reduce moisture and volatile acids that may bring unwanted flavors to the chocolate. Controlled to a certain point, conching also lowers viscosity by making the solid particles in suspension smaller and smoother. Like roasting, conching must be carefully timed. Rob Anderson, of Fresco Chocolate in Bellingham, Washington (US), offers consumers a way to taste the impact of roast and conche. For each batch of beans, Anderson varies roast and conche levels in different combinations, and notes those on packaging. For example, Anderson makes several bars with Papua New Guinea beans at 69 percent cocoa content. A "light roast, medium conche" results in "fruity, earthy" flavors. But those same beans with a "dark roast, medium conche" produce flavors of "caramalized [sic] brown sugar, roasted nuts, cherry." A "light roast, no conche" offers "lime, passion fruit, earthy" flavors.[9]

The next step, tempering, determines chocolate's appearance and shelf life. As with other materials that are tempered – for example, steel or glass – tempering chocolate involves a controlled temperature change combined with agitation to promote its strongest form. Cocoa butter fat can take six crystal forms, of which Form V is the ideal for chocolate. To generate Form V crystals, chocolate is melted to about 50° Celsius (122° Fahrenheit), and then cooled to about 27° Celsius (81° Fahrenheit), while being agitated. This typically happens in a machine, although confectioners sometimes temper by hand, often on a marble slab, using a spatula to constantly move the molten chocolate. A well-tempered bar will be glossy and durable, and makes a snapping sound when broken. Tempered chocolate stays so when it is stored at room temperature, although in hot climates, it is better off in the refrigerator. If chocolate goes through a temperature change – say, stored in a cupboard above a stove and then cooled back down in a fridge – it will go out of temper. The fat crystals lose their strong Form V, break apart, and rise to the top of the bar. This is called fat bloom, and it appears as a greasy, yellowish layer that smudges off easily. Bloomed chocolate is still edible and it is possible to re-temper it. Sugar bloom occurs when chocolate – which prefers dry storage – is exposed to moisture. In this case, sugar crystals rise to the surface, appearing as a grayish layer.

Tempered chocolate still has several steps to go. Still in molten form, it must be deposited into a mold shaped like the final bar; filled molds are usually vibrated to release any trapped air. Then they move through a cooling tunnel to harden the chocolate. Finally, the chocolate is removed from the mold and wrapped in its packaging. Et voilà: a chocolate bar.

Semi-finished products

In between cocoa and chocolate are the semi-finished or intermediate products, which are also traded in vast quantities. One is cocoa liquor: whole beans milled to semi-liquid form. Liquor can be separated into its component parts, which are the other two semi-finished products: cocoa butter and cocoa powder. A little more than half of each bean is natural fat, which is sold as cocoa butter; the rest comprises non-fat cocoa solids, sold as cocoa powder.

Of the three, cocoa butter is the most valuable. It is essential to making chocolate, and cosmetics and pharmaceutical makers employ its moisturizing properties, so it has a role in several industries. While it is possible to separate out small quantities of butter by hand, extracting it on a commercial scale requires a hydraulic press. Cocoa butter's trading price is a multiple of the cocoa futures price (see chapter 4), and can be much higher; in 2014, for example, butter reached nearly three times the price of beans.[10] While the issue of regulating how much cocoa butter needs to be in chocolate may sound mundane, it has been a highly politicized matter. This was especially so in the EU, whose member countries fought a "Chocolate War" over cocoa butter and its substitutes for two and a half decades.[11] As the naturally occurring fat of the bean, cocoa butter is chocolate's ideal fat. Depending on several factors (such as the ingredients it is mixed with), cocoa butter melts at right around or below the average human body temperature of 37° Celsius (98.6° Fahrenheit), which gives chocolate its luxurious feel in our mouths.[12] But because cocoa butter is expensive, manufacturers have lobbied to allow other fats in chocolate that play a similar role, called cocoa butter equivalents (CBEs). CBEs can also be used to raise chocolate's melting point, helping it stay solid in hotter climates. The most common CBE is palm oil – another politically charged crop, whose monocropping has caused environmental degradation, especially in Southeast Asia and also West Africa.

When Europe was forming its common market in the 1970s, countries had different regulations regarding CBEs. The six countries that came together to found what would

eventually become the EU did not permit CBEs in chocolate. Britain, Denmark, and Ireland, however, did allow
them. When the latter joined the common market, those
countries that did not allow CBEs were furious, as their
domestic manufacturers now had to contend with competi-
tor chocolates that relied upon cheaper ingredients. The
debate continued through 1997, when the EU finalized
regulations that allow up to 5 percent of chocolate's fat to
be CBEs, and still bear the name "chocolate." Australia and
New Zealand soon afterwards enacted the same standard.[13]
In the US, by contrast, if a product is sold as chocolate, it
can *only* contain cocoa butter and no CBEs (though manufacturers there have also lobbied for CBE inclusion). In
both the US and EU, if a product is going to be sold as
"chocolate flavored" or similar, it can contain other fats.

While not as contentious at the national level as CBEs,
white chocolate appears to be a controversial issue for some
consumers, judging by the frequency with which I am
asked whether it is "really" chocolate. Cocoa butter is the
only part of the cocoa bean used to make white chocolate, so
it lacks the non-fat cocoa solids that give regular chocolate
its color and flavor. Both the US and EU require this type of
chocolate to be labeled as "white chocolate," and to contain
a minimum of 20 percent cocoa butter; other ingredients
include dry milk solids and fat, sugar, and often vanilla.[14]

Pressing out cocoa butter from liquor leaves behind a
cake of non-fat cocoa solids. Ground into cocoa powder,
these solids are used across the confectionery industry to make chocolate-flavored cakes, brownies, cookies,
icing, and ice cream; a great deal of cocoa powder goes
into drinks. Because cocoa does not mix easily with other
ingredients, including water and milk, an alkaline agent is
typically added to beans, nibs, or liquor that are destined to
become cocoa powder (powder itself can also be alkalized).

This process was invented by a Dutch man, Coenraad van Houten, in 1828, and is thus known as Dutching. Dutching makes cocoa powder more neutral on the acid/basic scale, which helps particles disperse and suspend more easily and uniformly when mixed with other things. Dutching also changes color and flavor. Overall, Dutching turns cocoa powder darker but, depending on the type of bean, it can achieve anything from red to black. (Strains that grow in Cameroon, for example, are known for their red color.) Paradoxically, Dutching does not intensify chocolate flavor and may even reduce it but, because it darkens the powder, we may perceive Dutched cocoa as tasting more "chocolatey" (Nabisco's Oreo cookies are a great example).

From this close look at the industrial value chain, we can see that by the time cocoa beans reach even the stage of semi-finished products, they bear little noticeable relationship to their origins as the seeds of *Theobroma cacao*. This is part of the reason why cocoa's sociocultural and economic values diverged when it entered a global trade pattern. In Mesoamerica, different people were often responsible for cultivating, transporting, processing, and retailing cocoa, as is the case today. But in that context, cocoa beans were recognized as the source of the final consumable. The value chain never wholly isolated Mesoamerican farmers as growers of a primary commodity, even if they did not enjoy socioeconomic status as high as that of people who were buried with beans, for example, or received them as tribute. The farmers would at least have been familiar with cocoa drinks, and might even have had a tradition of partaking of cocoa in some form. This is still the case for many farmers today, in historical growing areas of Central and South America. But it is generally not the case outside of those regions, including for the approximately two million growers in West Africa, as well as farmers in Asia Pacific. For them, the capital-intensive chocolate manufacturing process is alienating. They remain at a physical and economic distance from both that process and the industrialized good it creates. The history of cocoa tariffs reveals, in part, why this is the case.

Cocoa and chocolate tariffs

Colonial tariffs
In the village of Asountaa in Ghana, I was discussing the local scarcity of chocolate with Mercy Asabea, a cocoa grower whose family had moved from Brong Ahafo to the Western region to take advantage of available farmland. From my observations of her healthy-looking trees and quantities of cocoa drying on tables in the sunshine, Mercy seemed to be making successful use of the eight acres of land she had inherited when her father died. She had just observed that it would be good for her village to have better access to chocolate when she suddenly flared, apparently angry. The target? Europe, and its drain of her country's resources.

"Ghana made Europe what it is," Mercy said. "Cocoa comes from Ghana. Timber – Ghana. Manganese – Ghana. Gold – Ghana. Everything – Ghana. We have every resource here, yet Ghanaians are not progressing at all." Afterwards, I thought about what might have prompted Mercy to connect the inaccessibility of chocolate in her village with the extraction of Ghana's resources. One possibility is the colonial history that "made Europe what it is" today. That we could see cocoa in every direction from where we sat in Asountaa, but no chocolate, was an enduring specter of imperialism. For Mercy, the colonial pull of resources out of her country not only had never ended, it continued to prevent Ghanaians from "progressing." There are many reasons why colonizing countries were able to transfer a wealth of resources from the Americas, Caribbean, Asia Pacific, and Africa to Europe over centuries. Here, I look at colonial tariffs to understand how we reached a scenario of cocoa abundance and chocolate scarcity in Asountaa.

William Gervase Clarence-Smith has studied how nation-states traded cocoa from the mid-eighteenth through the early twentieth century, when the ideology of mercantilism battled with that of liberalism. His work reveals that tariff structures of the period nearly always protected domestic chocolate industries, and occasionally laborers.[15] While countries in Latin America, the Caribbean, and sub-Saharan Africa did impose protective tariffs, by and large taxes shielded chocolate makers in the US and Europe. Historical evidence shows how France, Britain, Portugal, Spain, Belgium, and the Netherlands used tariffs to develop chocolate industries more effectively than did growing countries.

Mercantilism held that a nation-state should "capture" as large a share of international trade as possible to build up political economic power. Imperialist countries also protected their colonies, in ways that helped colonizers maintain control over resource extraction. Tariffs and quotas (limits on amounts of traded goods) rose and fell depending on the needs of colony and colonizer. Tariffs were especially high whenever European wars had depleted national treasuries that governments needed to replenish, a frequent occurrence during the conflict-ridden 1800s. Intra-continental rivalries – for example, between France and Britain – played out in trade regulations, especially for shipping routes, as most trade was by sea. Ships carrying cocoa were subject to a messy set of rules regarding where they could put into port and what sorts of goods they could carry. These prioritized colonial relationships and antagonized former colonies and European rivals. For example, Spain banned trade with all former colonies; Britain would not allow Spanish ships to bring non-British goods to its Caribbean colony of Trinidad; and no one was sure who, if anyone, was allowed to bring cocoa into Puerto Rico, where local demand outstripped production.[16]

In addition to regulating where and how cocoa could travel, tariffs encouraged ships to bring in cocoa from a country's own colonies. When cocoa arrived on a national ship from that same country's colonies, import tariffs were low or nil. When cocoa arrived from another country's colonies, or on another nation's ships, tariffs rose. France instituted a complicated tariff structure that made it easiest to bring cocoa from French colonies, on French ships, to France (see table 3.1). Portugal had a simpler policy: colonial cocoa arriving on a Portuguese ship was subject to no import duties, while any cocoa arriving on a foreign ship carried a 9.7 pence tax per pound. Such tariffs meant that it made less economic sense, for example, for a French ship to take cocoa from Portugal's colony in Brazil to a Portuguese port: the cargo would have been more profitable in France – a tax difference of 7.3 pence per pound. Given the choice, French ships would of course bring cocoa to France.

From about 1850, the Industrial Revolution brought

Table 3.1 French import duties on cocoa, early 1840s	
French cocoa import duties	British pence per pound
Colonial cocoa on French ship	1.1
Foreign Pacific cocoa on French ship	2.2
Foreign Atlantic cocoa on French ship	2.4
Foreign ship and overland	4.6

Source: Tariff figures from Clarence-Smith, *Cocoa and Chocolate*, 47.

significant changes to chocolate – and tariffs. Prior to manufacturing advances, value was added to cocoa by turning
it into expensive drinks. While these drinks were more
valuable than beans, they had a small consumer market
limited to a few social groups. With the invention of technologies to mass-produce cheap bars, capturing *chocolate's*
added value became a meaningful contributor to national
economies. Around the same time, the ideology of liberalism, which supported lessening or eradicating the
protectionist measures of mercantilism, gained ground.
From the 1850s, Clarence-Smith describes a "golden era
of free trade," during which cocoa "taxes and regulations
melted away like spring snow."[17] Britain did away with
differential import tariffs and imposed a straight penny
per pound tax no matter where cocoa originated. The US,
a rising world power, abolished all tariffs on cocoa beans
by 1886. Switzerland and the Netherlands established low
duty or duty-free cocoa imports that helped both build
chocolate industries, so much so that the Netherlands
became the world's largest grinder and remained so until
2014.

As cocoa tariffs fell, chocolate taxes became more important. While there was already some relatively large-scale
chocolate production in the US and Europe by the 1800s,
governments helped to grow domestic manufacturing
capacity even further by discouraging chocolate imports.
Early in that century, Britain banned imported chocolate while, in the late 1800s, the US increased tariffs on
imported chocolate. Perhaps because it had fewer colonial
holdings from which to extract cocoa, Germany focused its
efforts on making chocolate machinery. During this period,
growing countries, including Mexico and Costa Rica, did
impose protectionist measures to support local chocolate
industries, but such attempts were less common. For the

most part, tariff structures protected chocolate manufacturers in Europe and the US.

Because European countries had lowered tariffs on cocoa and reduced favoritism toward colonies, growers could now sell beans to anyone that wanted to buy them. Demand for chocolate was rising and, combined, these factors incentivized growers to produce more cocoa. But higher tariffs on chocolate were simply too high for growing countries to compete. Britain's import tax on chocolate, for example, was twice that of raw beans; this was too high for colonial growers, such as the Gold Coast, to meet, although not for Britain's European neighbors. The Industrial Revolution began in Britain, and spread rapidly to the continent and the young United States of America. These countries built industrial infrastructure as soon as such infrastructure became possible, and then protected it. Newly industrialized countries rarely shared manufacturing technologies with former or current colonies; instead, they maintained colonies as sources of inputs and as markets for finished goods. Because they were all industrializing – and maintaining empires – around the same time, European rivals could handle one another's chocolate import tariffs. Cocoa growing countries could not.

Tariffs today

Today, industrialized countries have scaled back tariffs on imported chocolate. For example, the US African Growth and Opportunity Act (AGOA), passed in 2000 and renewed until 2025, encourages sub-Saharan African countries that demonstrate "improvements" in enforcing the rule of law, human rights, and respect for labor standards to export goods to the US, including chocolate.[18] If a product meets AGOA eligibility standards, it may enter the US without being subject to import tariffs.[19] In 2014, the US International Trade Commission (USITC) reported on import changes since AGOA's implementation. In 2000, the US imported $4.4 million worth of products in the category "Cocoa, chocolate, and confectionery." By 2013, imports in that same category were valued at $122.8 million.

This is, at first glance, an astonishing rise and would appear to indicate that AGOA prompted a flourishing value-added industry in eligible African cocoa growing countries. However, in a footnote, the report indicates that "most of the U.S. imports from AGOA beneficiaries of products included in the cocoa, chocolate, and confectionery group consists of cocoa beans, which have an NTR duty rate of free and therefore do not enter under AGOA . . . provisions."[20] The increase in import value was due mainly to the rising price of cocoa, which went from a less than $900 per MT average in 2000 to a 2013 average of more than $2,400 per MT. While the value of liquor imports from Ivory Coast and Cameroon increased from 2000 to 2013 (in Ivory Coast's case, from zero), as did cocoa powder imports from Ghana and Ivory Coast (again from zero), Nigeria exported neither semi-finished product to the US. The only African country to make the report's chart for chocolate and confectionery exports – which have the most value added – was South Africa, which grows no cocoa at all. In 2013, all other AGOA eligible countries together exported a miniscule $327,000 worth of finished chocolate and confectionery to the US.

This evidence suggests that eliminating tariffs on value-added chocolate products has had an insignificant impact on African exports. While tariff structures played an important role in preventing growing countries from initially developing value-added processing capacity, they do not seem to be the primary determinant today. One alternative explanation is that once a country has become entrenched in the export of agricultural goods, which are not high revenue earners, it is difficult to make the expensive transition to manufacture. The complex machinery needed to make industrial bar chocolate raises entry barriers to value addition even higher. Another possibility is that this analysis involves only US imports from African countries; African value-added export volumes to Europe and Asia may be different. And, in fact, if we look at the wider map of value addition, we can see evidence of change from the historically strict divide between cocoa producing and chocolate making countries.

World map of value addition

The ICCO forecasts that the 2016–17 season cocoa crop will exceed 4.5 million MT, and that grindings will be more than 4.2 million MT.[21] Countries that grow cocoa will account for less than half of those grindings – 1.9 million MT – while cocoa importing regions will process the majority of beans.[22] Among the latter, Europe predominates, processing nearly twice the volume of any other region (see figure 3.1). Within Europe, the Netherlands is the leading processing country, followed by Germany.

This has been the global processing pattern since the invention of industrial bar chocolate. Part of the reason is the history of colonialism and tariffs. But there are other reasons, less to do with exploitative political economic arrangements and more to do with the material reality of the chocolate industry. Most important is the location of mature chocolate markets. By the time today's largest cocoa growers were rising to supply predominance, Europe and North America were firmly industrialized, and workers in those countries had both the taste for everyday luxuries

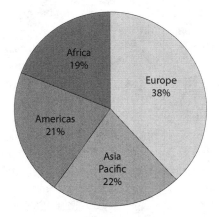

Figure 3.1 Cocoa grindings by region, 2016–2017 season forecast
Source: Statistics from *QBCS*, XLIII, table 3.

like chocolate and the means to buy them. Thus consumer markets for bar chocolate were, from the start, located at a considerable distance from origins. While chocolate does have a long shelf life (around two years for dark and one for milk, depending on inclusions), it requires a stable room temperature to avoid bloom and retain its most attractive form and texture. Without a reliable cool or cold chain, transporting chocolate to and from the tropical climates where cocoa grows runs a high risk of degrading it.[23] Add to that the relative ease with which countries in the Global North access other inputs, especially dairy for milk chocolate, and it was a sound logistical choice to establish chocolate factories within the countries and regions where the product would be distributed and sold. This does not, of course, diminish the economic loss that the world's largest cocoa growing region, West Africa, has experienced by exporting its crop mainly as an agricultural commodity. A 2013 Ecobank Research report, for example, noted that West Africa exports 74 percent of its cocoa as beans.[24]

Table 3.2 Top cocoa processing countries, 2016–2017 season forecast	
Country	World grindings share (%)
Ivory Coast	13.0
Netherlands	12.8
Germany	9.7
Indonesia	9.4
US	9.4
Brazil	5.3
Malaysia	5.0
Ghana	5.0
Spain	2.4
Singapore	2.0

Source: Statistics from QBCS, XLIII, table 3.

However, in the year after that report was published, a new development occurred. In the 2014–15 season, Ivory Coast processed more cocoa than the historical leader among processing countries, the Netherlands. While the ICCO estimates that Dutch companies processed the most cocoa in 2015–16, it forecasts that Ivory Coast will again take the lead in 2016–17.[25] This means that the world's largest cocoa *producing* country is now also the world's largest cocoa *processing* country (see table 3.2). This is a milestone to be celebrated, as it mitigates the historical tendency for major cocoa exporters to lose out on the full value of their crop.

But we must also read this changing processing landscape through a critical lens. When factory capacity expands, as it has in West Africa and Asia Pacific, it does not necessarily mean that cocoa power or politics have reversed. Producing countries may physically house processing facilities, but their governments do not usually own them. It is foreign multinationals that have increased grinding capacity at origins. Each of the three largest processors – Barry Callebaut, Cargill, and Olam, which together process about 60 percent of traded cocoa (see chapter 4) – has a manufacturing presence in the major producer countries. In 2015, Cameroon increased cocoa processing by 49 percent over 2014, thanks to two foreign companies: Sic Cacao, which is a local Barry Callebaut affiliate, and Chococam, owned by South Africa's Tiger Brand.[26] Barry Callebaut, which is headquartered in Switzerland, has factories in at least four of the top five exporters. In 2007, it doubled its processing capacity in Ghana and began a similar-sized expansion in Ivory Coast.[27] By 2013, five multinationals owned 86 percent of cocoa processing capacity in Ivory Coast.[28]

Public relations statements announcing expanded processing capacity suggest that the intention is to alleviate poverty in growing countries. For example, Barry Callebaut's 2007 "Expansion story" for Ghana described how doubling cocoa processing was "making a contribution to the economic development of this country."[29] Its announcement that same year of investment in processing facilities in Ivory Coast highlights building a new medical center for cocoa farmers in the village of Goh, about 60 kilometers (37 miles) from one of its factories. After observing West Africa's cocoa industry for two years for Reuters, journalist Órla Ryan described the many challenges of processing cocoa where it grows. From her account, we can add the following to the tariff and market location factors I've already described: having to depend on local bean supply rather than using different sources as a safeguard; the complex logistics of shipping liquor, butter, powder, and chocolate compared to the easier shipment of beans; and higher energy costs in growing countries, which lower labor costs barely offset (as today's chocolate factories don't require many workers).[30] Because it would be so much easier to ship beans to Europe and North America for processing, the altruistic motive of poverty alleviation rings hollow. Multinational companies do not take large investment decisions, such as setting up cocoa processing factories, because they want to help poor people. A more compelling economic rationale for increasing factory capacity in growing countries is because one particular cost is reduced: taxes.

Taxes and development

A main driver of increased manufacturing in developing countries – especially of electronics, toys, and textiles, and most visibly in East and Southeast Asia – in the late twentieth century was the expansion of tax-free or tax-reduced zones. When a company receives permission to operate in an export processing zone (EPZ) or free trade zone (FTZ), or under other reduced-tax auspices, the company typically pays no customs duties on inputs coming into its factory or on value-added products leaving it. To illustrate, say a foreign company built a cocoa factory in Ghana in a FTZ (as several have done). The company would not have to pay any duties on beans arriving from farms, or on liquor that it shipped out. A processor in the Netherlands, by contrast, would have to cover the cost of many possible taxes: Ghanaian export taxes on beans, Dutch import taxes on beans, Dutch export taxes on cocoa products leaving the Netherlands, and import taxes on those products when they arrive in another country. Because tariffs are typically calculated on the value of goods, those applied to the more expensive semi-finished or finished products can be more impactful on a company's bottom line. These would be export duties on chocolate or – more typically – import duties on chocolate coming into a country with its own manufacturers. Not all of these tariffs always apply but, by operating in an EPZ or FTZ, a manufacturer can avoid at least some of them.

Development depends upon a functional national infrastructure: roads, ports, telecoms, utilities, water and sanitation systems, and so forth. These are foundational to well-being and livelihood for all, and it is nearly impossible to fund them without a corporate tax base. Taxes from agricultural exports such as cocoa rarely translate into enough fiscal strength to support such infrastructure. So when Barry Callebaut claims that its new factories are "making a contribution to the economic development" of Ghana, or celebrates its new medical facility in Ivory Coast, the reality is that *unless the company is paying appropriate taxes*, it is not contributing in a meaningful way to development. In Ghana, Barry Callebaut's and Cargill's factories are both located in the Tema Free Zone Enclave.[31] In Ivory Coast, multinationals that introduced new processing capacity "benefited from fiscal incentives" – a euphemism for tax breaks.[32] Under these reduced- or no-tax schemes with Ivorian and Ghanaian governments, it is extremely doubtful that any company's processing presence will lead to noticeable, widespread improvement in everyday living. National accounts always appear more positive when journalists and corporate public relations announcements report increased processing capacity. But it is a mistake to conflate the fact of processing more cocoa with development for a country's population. That more beans are turned into liquor in Ghana or Cameroon *will not translate* into improved life circumstances, except perhaps for those fortunate enough to gain factory employment. But given the efficiencies of today's chocolate manufacture, these jobs are few. In Ghana – population 27 million –

Barry Callebaut's factory employed 100 people in 2005.[33] In 2007, the company's factory expansion in Ivory Coast – population 23 million – created around sixty new jobs.[34]

Finally, these facilities produce little chocolate. As illustrated, making chocolate is capital intensive and technically challenging; the process adds far more value to cocoa than making semi-finished products. By not manufacturing chocolate in growing countries, even the largest factories cannot boast that they offer local workforces the opportunity to command the full process of value addition. But even if they did, the question remains of whether and how this would benefit growers.

Processing potential

When I am in cocoa producing areas of Africa, growers often tell me that only white people overseas eat chocolate. I asked Afia Frempong, who farmed cocoa near the village of Fenaso Domeabra in Ghana, why this was so. She replied, "Because they are rich. And we are poor. People eat chocolate overseas . . . it's those people, the whites. Ghanaians don't know how to make the chocolate, so they have to provide the raw materials, the cocoa. But we don't know how to make chocolate."

Ghana *does* make chocolate. The state is partial owner of Cocoa Processing Company, which makes semi-finished products and Golden Tree chocolates, which are available domestically, especially in cities and larger towns.[35] Many people I meet in Ghana, particularly in urban locations, have heard of the brand. Food industry workers that I interviewed in Kumasi talked about their regular enjoyment of chocolate, including Golden Tree, and chocolate's role in celebrations and romantic relationships. As I noted in the introduction, Accra is now home to a craft chocolate company, '57 Chocolate.[36] Domestic chocolate exists, and people purchase, enjoy, and share it.

So then why did Afia state unequivocally that her country does not make chocolate? One possibility is the dynamics of conversation with a white American woman. Sometimes, I have noticed, people who live and work in Ghana's rural regions seem hyper-conscious of the disparity between my country's economic development and their own, in a way that young urbanites (such as the food industry workers I interviewed) do not seem to be. This may have prompted a more fatalistic interpretation of Ghana's industrial capacity than conversation with someone of a different race, gender, or nationality than me might have done. But even if that was the case, Afia seemed to be describing the lived experience of the word "alienated" that I used at the start of this chapter, to indicate that cocoa growers are distanced from cocoa processing and its final luxury product. Her comments suggest a world divided by race and industrial capacity, not unlike the perpetual colonial legacy that Mercy Asabea recognized when she stated that Europe had taken Ghana's resources, to the point where her country was "not progressing at all."

After Afia made her comment, I asked why Ghanaians did not know how to make chocolate, despite growing cocoa for more than a century. Her neighbor, Cecilia Nkansah, replied, "The machines are probably not made in Ghana. You need the machines." Afia agreed. "Over there you have machines to fashion these products," she added, "but over here we don't have these machines. We are not serious, we just send the cocoa to you."

Though Ghana has cocoa processing factories, little in the rural surroundings of Fenaso Domeabra suggested a domestic industrial base. The infrastructure that accompanies industry, including water and sanitation systems, power stations, and heavy transport, were not part of Afia's and Cecilia's everyday experiences in their village. Kim and Priscilla Addison of '57 Chocolate told me that it was easy to get high quality Ghanaian cocoa for their business. But when the sisters take samples of their chocolate to cocoa farmers, they say that the majority of them have never tasted it before.[37] Beans move out of rural areas, supplying chocolate makers large and small with their crucial input. But the reverse is not true on a large scale: industrial processing in Ghana does not return benefits to growing regions, at least to a noticeable extent for Afia or Cecilia.

Some five and a half hours away from their village by car, in the Tema Free Zone Enclave, a few people work wage-labor jobs to process cocoa. In contrast to the histories of Hershey and Cadbury companies, which built company towns that included housing, transportation, public recreation facilities, and so forth that brought material improvement to the lives of factory workers,[38] the cocoa processing industry in Ghana today is not a promising place to look for improving growers' lives. Structurally, there are few bidirectional links between processing facilities and the country's expansive rural regions. The presence of factories that pay little in taxes and offer few jobs seems only to perpetuate the alienation that Afia and Cecilia described. Though we can celebrate the national achievement of increased processing capacity, we cannot look to in-country value addition as a source of material benefits for growers.

This is one illustration of how economic power concentrates within a limited space in the cocoa industry. The next chapter continues this analysis, looking at how and where economic and other types of power reside in the world of cocoa.

CHAPTER FOUR

Power in the Market

Where power lies in the cocoa market is central to its geopolitics. While much industry power is concentrated in the Global North, no force operates in a vacuum, and every entity in the value chain works in relationship with others that have comparatively more or less influence. For example, the world's largest manufacturers and processors have the power to mitigate price risk and protect their own bottom lines, whereas farmers generally do not. Because they buy most of the world's cocoa, the largest processors have power over nation-states that export it. But governments in turn have power over growers, and have both supported and abused them through cocoa politics. Since the late twentieth century, nearly all governments have been subject to the prevailing ideology of neoliberalism, which has impacted their ability to regulate domestic markets and politicized cocoa in new ways. This chapter explores each of these forces, but it begins with the power of brand association: the ideas that may form in a consumer's mind about chocolate before she or he even takes a bite of a bar. While Asian markets have become important for the growth potential of multinational chocolate companies, to understand brand entrenchment, we must look closely at mature chocolate markets.

Big brands

Walk through the candy aisle of a grocery store in North America or Europe, and the vast array of chocolate shapes, sizes, and colors seems to offer a lot of choice. In the post-Fordist vein of diversifying product features (see chapter 8), chocolates now morph seasonally and cater to various "needs." Hershey's Kisses, for example, come wrapped in colored foil to match holiday themes, and Mars's M&M's are not only available in almond, crispy, dark, mint, peanut, peanut butter, and pretzel (among others), they can be ordered in special colors and even imprinted with specific images. Behind this crowd of chocolates, however, there are few companies. Globally, many companies make confectionery but, among them, just five focus on chocolate and dominate the mature markets of Europe and North America: Mars, Mondelēz, Ferrero, Nestlé, and Hershey (see table 4.1). Due to their predominance, but also the strength of their brands, author Lawrence L. Allen calls these companies the Big Five.[1] While Mondelēz is not a recognizable name for chocolate, it owns Cadbury brands, which are well known. In 2010, Kraft Foods acquired Cadbury; in 2012, Kraft split into two companies and the confectionery business, including Cadbury, became Mondelēz International.

These five companies capture a third of the value of all industrially made confections. If we narrow that to chocolate, whose 2016 global market value was $100 billion, their share jumps to nearly two-thirds (see table 4.2). With revenues well into billions of dollars, the financial power of these companies is great. To make a comparison, Mars's 2015 net sales equaled a little more than half of Ivory Coast's 2015 gross domestic product (GDP) of $31.8 billion.[2] If these proportions stay constant, then every two

Table 4.1 Largest chocolate companies by revenue, 2015		
Company	Country	Net sales ($million)
Mars Inc.	US	18,480
Mondelēz International	US	14,350
Ferrero Group	Italy	10,911
Nestlé SA	Switzerland	10,466
Meiji Co. Ltd.	Japan	9,818
The Hershey Company	US	7,485
Lindt & Sprüngli AG	Switzerland	4,022
Arcor	Argentina	3,500
Ezaki Glico Co. Ltd.	Japan	3,049
August Storck KG	Germany	2,272

Source: Figures from http://www.candyindustry.com/2015-Global-Top-100-Part-4; I excluded companies that do not manufacture chocolate primarily.

Table 4.2 Big Five chocolate companies, market share, 2015		
Company	Confectionery market share (% of $183.5 billion)	Chocolate market share (% of $100 billion)
Mars Inc.	10.1	18.5
Mondelēz International	7.8	14.4
Ferrero Group	5.9	10.9
Nestlé SA	5.7	10.5
The Hershey Company	4.1	7.5
Total Big Five	*33.6*	*61.8*

Source: I calculated market shares using figures from table 4.1.

years, Mars earns more than the value of *all* goods and services exchanged in the world's largest cocoa producer. And we can expect at least some of these Big Five sales figures to rise, in part due to India and China. In India, chocolate consumption nearly tripled between 2005 and 2013, and is predicted to more than double by 2019.[3] Just two companies command over three-quarters of India's near $1 billion market: Cadbury brands capture 62 percent and Nestlé, 18 percent.[4]

There is an emotional power that comes with predominance by so few. Cumulatively, the effect of their brand repetition is that chocolate itself may become understood, categorically, as the products made by these companies. In the US, for example, Milton S. Hershey was the first to market milk chocolate bars on a large scale, and Hershey's brands quickly came to dominate. Only Mars has rivaled Hershey domestically and, for a time, Mars sourced its chocolate from Hershey.[5] Thus Hershey's flavor, somewhat sour in comparison to other brands, became the flavor of US chocolate. This is not to say that every American prefers Hershey's. Rather, when a flavor leads a market so successfully, chocolate can become conflated with it. Similarly in Britain, there were initially three major competitors: Fry's (established 1761), Cadbury (established 1824), and Rowntree (established 1862). In 1919, Fry's merged with Cadbury, and Switzerland-based Nestlé acquired Rowntree in 1988. Cadbury began to dominate Britain's market with the launch of Dairy Milk in 1905, the first mass-produced milk chocolate in the UK. With the enormous line of products that followed, including Fruit & Nut and Whole Nut bars, Roses, Flake, and Creme Eggs, Cadbury established a British national palate for its caramel-sweet milk chocolate.

With the exception of Ferrero, each of the Big Five has been around for a century or more (nearly two hundred years for Cadbury), and enjoys the power of entrenchment. Because they established supremacy by offering consistent flavor, recent innovations have been for the most part superficial. As craft makers introduce novel flavors and textures, however, the Big Five are responding by acquiring companies that offer distinct chocolate experiences: for example, Mars acquired Dove brand, and Hershey bought Dagoba Organic Chocolate and Scharffen Berger. While such acquisitions signal responsiveness to changing tastes, they do not alter core practices. They also keep the vast system of bulk cocoa production intact (see chapter 7). Quality requirements for bulk cocoa help to ensure that beans are as clean and homogenous as possible, so that manufacturers can easily blend crops to achieve their brand flavors. Quality controls are not about cultivating unique flavor potential, retaining genetic diversity, or reducing negative environmental impacts. Outside of initiatives directed specifically at these goals, the industry's continued reliance upon bulk cocoa for consistent brand flavors gives growers little incentive to act upon other priorities. And, for so many consumers, the experience of chocolate endures as the experience of a handful of brands.

Invisible players

There is another segment of industry players that, though seldom discussed, are in some ways even more influential in cocoa's trade than chocolate manufacturers. These are the processors, also called grinders. Near the close of the twentieth century, about forty companies processed sizable amounts of cocoa. Then, over about two decades, a series of acquisitions resulted in just three commanding majority market share. By 2015, Barry Callebaut, Cargill, and Olam were grinding about 60 percent of all traded cocoa.[6] Processors buy cocoa beans and manufacture them to liquor, powder, and butter, as well as chocolate (see chapter 3). They supply not only the Big Five (Olam sells to at least four of those companies, and Barry Callebaut makes chocolate for Nestlé, Mondelēz, and Hershey), but also confectioners, bakers, pastry chefs, caterers, and food companies. Barry Callebaut, for example, supplies Unilever, the world's third largest consumer goods company and maker of, among others, Ben & Jerry's ice cream, with 70 percent of its cocoa and chocolate. Processors link the vast system of cocoa cultivation to the cakes, cookies, ice cream, brownies, pastries, drinks, and other sweets that rely on chocolate's unique flavor.

The leader is Barry Callebaut. With headquarters in Switzerland, the company is the result of a 1996 merger between Cacao Barry of France and Callebaut of Belgium, joining industry knowledge from three countries with long chocolate histories. In 2013, Barry Callebaut purchased the Cocoa Ingredients Division of Petra Foods. Based in Singapore, Petra had been Asia's largest cocoa supplier, with sales in excess of $1 billion at the time of purchase. The capacity that Barry Callebaut gained from this acquisition made it the world's largest cocoa processor, with about 25 percent of grindings.[7] Among the Big Three processors, as we might call them, only Barry Callebaut has a consumer presence. It represents itself as a *chocolate* company rather than as a cocoa processor (though making chocolate is only one part of its business),[8] and is sometimes in a positive media spotlight for this reason.[9] The company's website features multimedia content about the process of chocolate making, as well as products for manufacturers, confectioners, and chefs. Callebaut TV offers technical tutorials, while amateurs and professionals alike can train in twenty Callebaut Chocolate Academy centers across Europe, North America, and Asia Pacific.

In contrast, the second and third largest processors have virtually no public face for chocolate. Cargill, the largest private corporation in the US by revenue, describes its business as providing "food, agriculture, financial and industrial products and services to the world."[10] The company trades

in beef, turkey, oils, salt, metals, ethanol, starches, phar-
maceuticals, and ocean and land transportation services,
among many other things. In 2015, Cargill finalized its
$440 million purchase of the chocolate business of Archer
Daniels Midland (ADM), which gave it about a 19 percent share of cocoa grindings.[11] Around the same time,
ADM sold its cocoa business to Singapore-based Olam
International for $1.3 billion, making Olam not only one
of the largest cocoa sourcing companies, but also the third
largest processor with a 16 percent market share.[12] Olam,
which began in 1989 exporting cashews from Nigeria to
India, now describes itself as "a leading agri-business operating from seed to shelf in 70 countries."[13]

While Barry Callebaut, Cargill, and Olam are familiar
names in the cocoa industry, media accounts of chocolate seldom mention them. When an article, book, website,
or blog post is concerned with trade justice, it usually
points the proverbial finger at the Big Five. For example,
using data from *Cocoa Barometer 2015*, the website Make
Chocolate Fair! breaks down the price of chocolate into proportions that different supply chain actors receive.[14] While
the illustration shows that grinders receive 7.6 percent of
bar price, the text does not name them. A different illustration does name the Big Five, with their percentage of global
confectionery sales. A reader might reasonably conclude
that these chocolate companies are linked to farmers' low
remuneration, without learning about the role of cocoa
processors. Similarly, in 2013, UK-based charity Oxfam
issued the first scorecards for its Behind the Brands initiative, which assessed the "biggest food companies' policies
on issues from water to women . . . and what they do to
measure and improve their impact on every worker and
farmer who makes their ingredients."[15] Nestlé, Mars, and
Mondelēz each received a scorecard, but no processor did.

Organizations and journalists are right to draw attention to major chocolate companies. Because they depend upon brand loyalty, these companies are more likely to respond to consumer calls for trade justice – and, indeed, they have (see chapter 6). But exclusive focus on them leaves some of the most powerful industry players to operate in relative invisibility. The Big Five generally have higher sales figures than the largest processors, because they capture brand value. However, each of Barry Callebaut, Cargill, and Olam *processes more cocoa* annually than any of the Big Five or, indeed, any other enterprise. They thus have a tremendous vested interest in keeping cocoa supply abundant and its price low. While processors cannot individually move price up or down in any significant way (nor can chocolate manu-facturers), their scale affords them the power of impressing these priorities across the cocoa industry.

Power over price

As with all commodities, cocoa's price rises and falls, sometimes unexpectedly. Because cocoa and chocolate both have seasons,[16] and because only a few countries grow cocoa in large volumes, cocoa has inherent short-term price volatility. In other words, supply and demand fluctuate throughout the year and, with them, price. Unlike oil, dia-monds, or coffee, whose major producers have (at least at times) collaborated to control supply and therefore price, the cocoa industry has never maintained a producer con-sortium. In the early 1980s, the ICCO introduced a price control system based on a buffer stock, which planned to withhold cocoa from the world market during years of abundant supply (thus helping to avoid a price fall), and release those reserves when needed. However, the scheme was abandoned in the late 1990s, leaving cocoa without a global stabilization body.[17] In the late 1980s, Ivory Coast, then newly the world's largest producer, attempted to control price on its own by withholding stocks, but this too had little impact.[18]

Consumption factors influence price, sometimes dramatically, as when the swift and sustained rise in chocolate demand in the late nineteenth century put upward pressure on price. Today, reports that the largest processors and manufacturers are grinding more or less cocoa than expected send cocoa's world market price up or down. Production factors, of course, are also influential. This does not mean that *farmers* determine price; rather, the forces that farmers are subject to – such as weather and politics – influence it. The main determinants of cocoa's world market price are weather, crop health, and political stability in major producer countries; prices of other commodities; and chocolate demand and political economic events in major consumer countries. Another important factor is stocks: how much cocoa is stored in (mainly European) warehouses from previous seasons.

Though these influences are not necessarily connected to each other – the weather in Ivory Coast, for example, is unrelated to desire for chocolate in Britain – when it comes to cocoa's price, they are imbricate: they intertwine and overlap, influencing price in complex relation to one another. However, there are *trends* for single factors. In general, as for any good, limited supply and increased demand drive price up, while abundant supply and weak demand drive it down. Human predictions – things that people *believe* will happen – also shift price.

Because so much emphasis is put on cocoa's low price as a driver of poverty, it can be easy to interpret price rises as being unequivocally positive for growers. But it is important to remember that when cocoa's price does rise, it means that either demand has grown faster than expected or, more likely, supply has fallen. Sometimes supply drops because farmers abandon cocoa; at other times, it falls because farmers are suffering a decline in productivity. The relationship between supply and price does not allow all farmers to grow more cocoa *and* enjoy a sustained high price. If cocoa's price were to rise very high, it would likely be because many farmers had suffered a dramatic loss of their chief livelihood.

Weather

A healthy cocoa yield depends upon, among other things, the right mix of rain and sunshine. Weather in West Africa matters most for cocoa's world market price, especially the two largest producers, Ivory Coast and Ghana. While the Caribbean island of Grenada produces high-value flavor beans, its crop is too small to register a strong influence upon world market price. Unseasonable local weather may impact production for the Grenada Chocolate Company,[19] but cocoa's world market price will not respond as it would to, say, drought in Ivory Coast.

In addition to rainy and dry periods, analysts pay attention to West Africa's harmattan, the windy season that occurs from around late November through March. Harmattan winds originate in the Sahara Desert and blow southwards across the Sahelian semi-desert region, filling the air with dusty grit all the way to the Atlantic coast. The resulting haze can be so intense that it blocks sunlight and lowers temperatures, both of which can harm the cocoa crop. A strong or sustained harmattan – or any unseasonable weather in West Africa – typically means a poor harvest and thus lower supply. In contrast to global food prices (as well as that of oil), which had been falling since about 2012, cocoa remained high from 2013 through mid-2016,

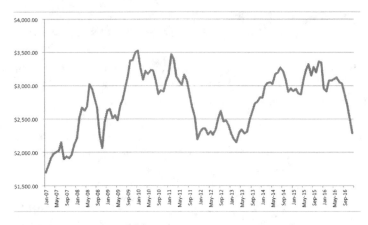

Figure 4.1 Cocoa monthly price averages, 2007–2016

Source: Price data from ICCO, https://www.icco.org/statistics/cocoa-prices/monthly-averages.html.

supported by predicted and actual occurrences of bad weather in West Africa. In particular, the El Niño cycle from March 2015 to June 2016 intensified poor weather, keeping upward pressure on price (see figure 4.1).

Conflict

Civil conflict in Ivory Coast since the late 1990s has also contributed to cocoa's high price. The politics of land ownership, particularly for migrant farmers, is at the heart of the conflict (see chapter 5). A particularly troubled period occurred from 1999 through late 2004. In 1999, about 20,000 migrant farmers were forced out of the southwest cocoa regions; by 2003, the number of displaced was around 100,000.[20] While media attention focused on national-level conflict, including one successful (1999) and one failed (2002) coup d'état, as political scientist Matthew Mitchell points out, rural cocoa regions saw intense violence. As a result, cocoa's price rose to its highest in sixteen years. After this came a period of relative peace, but fighting escalated again in 2010 and 2011, around a disputed presidential election. The candidate from the northern, mainly Muslim region, Alassane Ouattara, was declared the winner, but allies of incumbent President Laurent Gbagbo, representing the southern, mainly Christian region, declared the results invalid and Gbagbo remained in office. In effect, Ouattara controlled the northern half of the country, Gbagbo the south, and the two carried out their political conflict in part through cocoa exports.

Ouattara, whom most world leaders recognized as the election's winner, banned cocoa exports to prevent Gbagbo from benefiting from export taxes. Some large buyers respected the ban, while others did not. Because the previous season had been abundant, there were plenty of cocoa stocks, which normally would help keep price low. However, Ouattara's export ban had the potential to limit future supply, particularly if cocoa piling up in Ivory Coast spoiled. In response, cocoa's price rose 15 percent, to its highest level in thirty years.[21] As conflict escalated, Ouattara declared that any company that exported during his ban would lose its license once he took office. This pushed cocoa's price even higher.[22] It fell in April 2011 and then stabilized briefly, when Gbagbo was removed and Ouattara assumed the presidency.

Unexpected influences
With Ivory Coast in a tenuous peace, unexpected factors continue to influence cocoa's price. At the start of 2016, bad weather had led to poor crop predictions for Ivory Coast and Ghana. But then both countries harvested more than expected. At the same time, Barry Callebaut issued a report that, while indicating robust sales for the company, cited a nearly 4 percent drop in chocolate sales globally in late

2015.[23] Now, the combination of higher-than-anticipated supply and a report of falling demand drove cocoa's price down. The impact was brief, however, as weather continued to be poor in West Africa. In particular, the 2015–16 harmattan was the strongest in thirty years. It began early and, just at the point when it would typically end, the winds strengthened, destroying delicate cocoa flowers and cherelles (baby pods). This led to predictions that Ivory Coast's mid-crop, harvested from around May through August, could be up to 200,000 MT lower than the year prior,[24] and cocoa's price went up again.

A few months later, in June, an unrelated incident caused another brief spike. This was the unexpected vote for Brexit, whereby the UK would secede from the EU. While Brexit will have wide-ranging economic impacts, the most immediate and spectacular was the drop in value of the British pound. After the vote, sterling fell to its lowest levels in more than thirty years. Unlike other commodities, cocoa's trading price correlates more closely with pounds than US dollars, and it is one of the few commodities still traded on the London exchange as well as in New York. Cocoa futures contracts are thus valued in either pounds or dollars.[25] As with the pound itself, after the Brexit vote, cocoa contracts denominated in pounds fell in value relative to dollar contracts. Because pounds had become cheaper compared to dollars, anyone using dollars could purchase contracts on the London exchange more cheaply than before the referendum; this pushed up the price of sterling contracts.

Brexit's impact was minor and brief, however, compared to the next unexpected turn of events. Estimates had generally agreed that cocoa's price would stay high, as chocolate demand was expected to outstrip supply. For example, in a 2014 report, the ICCO had predicted a price of about $3,800 per MT by the 2022–3 season.[26] Using comprehensive modeling, econometrician Christopher L. Gilbert put the most likely price for the 2020–1 season at \$5,000 per MT, in a book chapter published in 2016.[27] Gilbert stressed that it would be unwise to accept his prediction as anything more than an educated guess. But reading his assessment in early 2016, when supply was low and demand predicted to grow, it seemed to me entirely possible that the price would rise that high. Gilbert, however, was correct to caution readers. Starting in mid-2016, cocoa's price began a dramatic fall. The steep slide on the right-hand side of the chart in figure 4.1 has only kept going downwards. At the end of April 2017, the London futures price was £1,495, and the New York price was \$1,885 – prices not seen since early 2007. It turns out that high price predictions were – at least temporarily, and maybe in the long term – wrong.

Futures

In July 2010, Anthony Ward, co-founder of the London-based hedge fund and trading company Armajaro, paid over \$1 billion (£658 million) to buy 241,000 MT of cocoa beans, sparking outrage among commodities traders. To put this amount of cocoa in perspective, it was more than the 2015–16 estimated crops of Ecuador or Nigeria. At the time, it was about 7 percent of world supply, enough to make more than five billion quarter-pound chocolate bars.[28] Ward's purchase was contentious because it was vast, but also because he took physical delivery of the beans. Reporters routinely characterized it as an attempt to corner the market by hoarding cocoa until its price rose to Ward's satisfaction. Others saw the purchase as an exaggerated instance of the bets that traders place every day on commodities. The fact that Ward, who does not make chocolate, took physical shipment of the beans was unusual, but placing a large bet on a future price rise was not. This is because there are two ways that cocoa is traded: on physical markets (also called spot markets or cash markets) and on futures markets (also called terminal markets). While futures contracts call for physical delivery of beans, it is possible to settle them before the delivery date, which means no cocoa actually changes hands. In these instances, one way of thinking about a futures contract is as an exchange of bets on price, where cocoa is the betting medium. As the name implies, futures exchanges allow buyers and sellers to signal to one another what they believe will happen to the price of cocoa *in the future*.

Chocolate and confectionery companies use futures trading to hedge against price rises (hence they are called hedgers). For example, Chocolate Company believes the price of cocoa is going to rise – say, around the holiday season. The company will need cocoa at the holidays, but does not want to pay the higher price it expects at the time. So, Chocolate Company buys futures contracts for the amount of cocoa it will need, which lock in price and date of delivery. The seller of those contracts, Cocoa Company, now has a guaranteed price at which it will sell. The transaction has been helpful for both companies: by fixing price and amount in advance, both can budget realistically.

Anyone who trades futures must set up a margin account, into which they deposit a portion of contract value (typically 5 to 10 percent) to cover potential losses. Margin accounts are settled every trading day, meaning that as price goes up and down, gains and losses are recorded in margin accounts. If cocoa's price rises, Chocolate Company has the positive difference from the contract price deposited into its margin account every day. In contrast, Cocoa Company would have to cover a loss each day. Notice that one party – buyer or seller – must "win" and the other must "lose."

If Chocolate Company profits by $10,000 on its futures contracts, then Cocoa Company loses $10,000 against its contracts. We call this a zero-sum game, and it is true for all futures trading, not just cocoa.

The two companies settle their futures contracts in advance of delivery date, and then do their physical buying and selling of beans on the cash market, at what is called the spot price. If Chocolate Company predicted correctly and cocoa's price had been rising, so that profits were deposited into its margin account each day, then when Chocolate Company buys physical cocoa, it has *made up for the price rise* through those profits on the futures contracts. This is known as offsetting risk: profits from futures trading cancel out a price rise on the cash market. If this seems the opposite of intuitive, remember that Chocolate Company *benefited from the price rise*, because its futures contract locked in a lower price for cocoa. Cocoa Company *lost out on the price rise*, because it agreed to sell futures contracts for less than the cocoa turned out to actually be worth.

Anyone can buy and sell futures contracts, not just cocoa and chocolate companies. When a person buys futures without intending to use the commodity, she or he is called a non-commercial trader or speculator. Speculators enter the futures exchange to gamble on price changes. If the speculator believes the price will rise, she or he buys futures contracts, and then sells them if the price does go up (and before the delivery date). If the speculator believes the price will fall, she or he *sells* contracts at the current (presumably higher) price, then *buys contracts back* if the price falls, profiting from the difference.

Cocoa contracts are standardized so that each is worth 10 MT of beans. On the London exchange, cocoa prices move in £1 increments (meaning no pence are involved), and in New York, in $1 increments (meaning no cents are involved). Because each contract is worth 10 MT, each time cocoa's price shifts by £1/$1 per MT, contracts gain or lose £10/$10. To illustrate how people make money from this, let's say that I believe the price of cocoa is going to rise. In July, I purchase ten December contracts on the New York exchange, at $3,000 per MT. In December, I am proven correct, and the price has risen to $3,100. I sell my ten contracts and make a $10,000 profit:

$$\text{\$100 price increase per MT (\$3,100} - \text{\$3,000)}$$
$$\times \text{\$10 per contract} \times \text{10 contracts} = \text{\$10,000}$$

If I was wrong, and the price went down by $100, I would lose $10,000. This is a simplified version of what actually happens, but it captures the fundamentals of futures trading.

While cocoa's utility is irrelevant to the speculator, betting successfully on futures still depends on having commodity expertise. We would expect a chocolate company to employ staff to follow market trends, but speculators must also gain commodity-specific knowledge to place educated bets. Anthony Ward's firm, Armajaro (which was purchased by the trading house Ecom in 2014), has cocoa buying operations in Ivory Coast, Indonesia, and Ecuador. Through these, Ward has access to on-the-ground information in all major growing regions.[29] To be fair, Ward does not only use his extensive information system to profit from cocoa trading: Armajaro has made significant investments in supply chain traceability, and the World Bank took a stake in the trading firm in 2012 to support Armajaro's sustainability efforts.[30] A 2016 trading overview notes plans for a $142 million investment in a cocoa supply chain "that connects farmer to customer," with an emphasis on flavor bean production in Peru.[31] But as with his large cocoa purchase,

Ward's information access exaggerates a regular feature of the speculative market. Working in global financial sectors, speculators *all* have access to information about cocoa's price influences. Unlike Ward, they do not typically use this information to invest in traceability or support flavor cocoa production. Instead, speculators use the information to make trades for personal gain. In contrast, cocoa farmers are typically unable to access information beyond local weather and political conditions. We can take this as an important illustration of the fact that "the market" comprises individual people acting in their own, or a company's, interest. Cocoa's price is set not by invisible laws of nature, but by people making use of available information, and placing bets for their own purposes.

State versus market power

In his Resources volume *Coffee*, Gavin Fridell makes a powerful critique of capitalism and hegemonic ideals of "free trade" by illustrating *coffee statecraft*: how nation-states have shaped the coffee trade. This contrasts with neoliberal ideology – accepted by, among others, the World Bank, International Monetary Fund (IMF), and World Trade Organization (WTO) – that governments should limit or eliminate involvement in trade. Fridell argues that states have always set the terms for coffee trade and still do today. While the term "cocoa statecraft" would be too strong, certain nation-states do stand out for the prominent role their governments have played in the industry, and in politicizing cocoa. To illustrate, I address key features of cocoa governance in Ghana and Ivory Coast. Here, power is not over chocolate's identity (as with brands), supply chain priorities (as with grinders), or price (as with weather or futures). Instead, states have power over growers.

Ghana: postcolonial state-building

From the time of its introduction to Africa, cocoa has been of interest to the state. While the savvy of Gold Coast farmers in choosing to grow cocoa in the early twentieth century is clear, they were also newly subject to colonial tax regimes (see chapter 2). Because subsistence farming does not bring in much cash, farmers faced little choice but to expand export crop production to pay taxes. When the Gold Coast became the first colony in sub-Saharan Africa to win independence in 1957 and changed its name to Ghana, its agricultural economy and fiscal structure remained largely unchanged. Cocoa taxes were still crucial to the postcolonial state. At the time, Ghana exported more cocoa than any other country (cocoa remains among its top three exports, with crude petroleum and gold). As a major source of state revenue, cocoa has been highly politicized by virtually every government since independence.[32]

Cocoa taxes were central to the state-building efforts of Kwame Nkrumah, Ghana's first prime minister and president. A pan-African visionary, Nkrumah's speeches emphasized Africa's richness in both human and physical resources. At independence, he called upon Ghanaians as laborers, asking them to work hard alongside him to achieve economic freedom, now that political freedom was theirs. Industrialization was central to Nkrumah's vision and his most ambitious project was the Akosombo Dam. When completed, the dam contained the Volta River, flooding its basin and creating the largest artificial lake in the world. It was intended to provide hydroelectric power to Ghana and neighboring countries, driving an aluminum smelter and the construction of railroads and other heavy infrastructure; the lake itself was meant to house a transportation system and fishing industry. In short, the dam was the project upon which Nkrumah staked the building of Ghana.

But cocoa helped build the dam. While funding came from Britain, the US, Russia, and the World Bank, state cocoa revenues were also a source of financing. Given the importance – and cost – of Nkrumah's ambition, his government did not enjoy a smooth relationship with farmers. At the time, the Ashanti region was the leading domestic cocoa producing area (today it is the Western region). Nkrumah's government considered the Ashanti people a threat to his power and instituted oppressive policies that limited legal mechanisms to oppose his rule.[33] Another way to check Ashanti influence was to set a low producer price for cocoa, which is the price farmers receive after various costs are deducted (see chapter 5). In the early years of independence, through about 1965 (the period of the dam's construction), world market prices for cocoa fell. Of this already low price, Nkrumah's government retained up to half. The state did face many financial challenges: to start, there was cocoa's low price, but the government was also responsible for providing farmers with increasingly expensive inputs and supports, and it needed revenues for development projects, the dam most prominent among them. Nkrumah had staked his leadership and Ghana's future on a vision of industrialization and regional predominance. The economics of his plans meant that his government taxed cocoa farmers to the limit, but ultimately this cost both Nkrumah and growers. In 1966, Nkrumah was ousted in a coup d'état. By that time, farmers were abandoning cocoa, switching to food crops to support themselves. Even without heavy taxation, cocoa's sustained low price at the time would likely have motivated farmers to move away from the crop. But Nkrumah's use of cocoa as a political tool no doubt exacerbated the process, weakening the agricultural heart of Ghana's economy.

Ghana: partial liberalization
Though African states made robust development strides after independence, their capacity to undertake the kind of infrastructure and development projects that Nkrumah envisioned has diminished. Cocoa exporting states wield power over farmers, but their dependence on primary commodities means they are not powerful players in the world context. They are more likely to be beholden to the ideological beliefs and even whims of industrialized countries, as well as mandates from supranational organizations – mainly the World Bank, IMF, and WTO – that set terms for trade, governance, and development. After Nkrumah's tenure ended, global economic ideology swung away from favoring state-led development to neoliberalism. When the World Bank and IMF adopted this ideology, they began "exporting" neoliberal policies to the Global South through SAPs.

As did most postcolonial states, Ghana had amassed substantial debt by the late 1970s – just as cocoa prices plummeted again. Lower prices meant less state revenue, which made it increasingly difficult for Ghana to make payments on its debt. Under the leadership of Flight Lieutenant Jerry Rawlings (who led a successful coup d'état in 1981, superintended Ghana's transition to constitutional democracy in 1993, and served as president until 2001), the government turned to the "lenders of last resort," the IMF and World Bank. They are called this because, in exchange for loans, these banks make political demands of borrowing countries. During the 1980s and 1990s, the Bank and Fund demanded that borrowers adopt SAPs, which rolled back state involvement in agriculture, health services, the financial sector, and so forth. Among other cost-cutting measures, state agencies were required to fire employees and reduce salaries, and to cut subsidies on food and fuel.

At the same time, SAPs encouraged export production to increase state revenue. They were implemented identically in every borrowing country, regardless of context and heedless of necessary supports for *people*. Researchers and analysts have since heavily criticized these macroeconomic policies for their disproportionately negative impacts on women and children, as well as the poor and other marginalized groups.

To comply with SAPs and receive its loans (which were needed to pay back *other* loans), Ghana's state marketing board, Cocoa Board (often referred to as COCOBOD), was forced to make sweeping staff and budget cuts (as was virtually every other marketing board across the Global South). In addition, in 1992, Ghana partially liberalized its domestic market. Whereas before, the state was the only buyer, through its Produce Buying Company (PBC), now other companies were allowed to purchase cocoa from farmers. Since then, Ghana's cocoa output has risen, which was the intention of structural adjustment. Because of this, the World Bank often points to Ghana as a SAP success story. However, adjustment was not by itself responsible for increased exports, or for any benefits that farmers may have enjoyed since. While debt forced successive administrations to accept SAPs, Ghana alone among major cocoa exporters *resisted* the IMF and World Bank, and continued to regulate and resource its industry to a remarkable extent. In my fieldwork, I have observed a productive tension between liberalization and state control. This does not mean they work hand in hand; indeed, they are often in conflict. Nevertheless, the market's liberalized elements can offer innovations for production and, in some cases, farmer well-being, *because* the state maintains a protective infrastructure for the industry.

Any company wishing to buy cocoa in Ghana must

meet COCOBOD's licensing terms, and about two dozen such licensed buying companies, or LBCs, currently operate. Ghana's liberalization is described as partial because, while LBCs now compete with PBC for domestic purchasing, they all sell their cocoa to COCOBOD, which has sole right to export it. (There are exceptions for certified cocoa, including Fairtrade.) It is also because COCOBOD retained the power to set producer price. This gives Ghanaian farmers an advantage in sales transactions: they know how much LBCs must legally pay them. In recent decades, COCOBOD has offered farmers a higher portion of the world market price than during the punishing Nkrumah era; they currently receive about 70 percent of FOB price (see chapter 5). The state also assumes short-term price risk. If world market price rises significantly during a season, the government compensates farmers through a bonus. But if world market price falls, farmers still receive the set price. Because Ghana produces the best bulk beans, its high-grade cocoa trades at a premium. The government has a vested interest in its farmers' superior husbandry, and COCOBOD thus guards quality far more diligently than other major exporters.

Within this state support system, however, private LBCs rejuvenated a buying landscape that PBC had long monopolized. Though some areas continue to be served by just one buyer, many farmers can now choose among several LBCs. If it has a buying presence in the area, one possible sales outlet is the farmer-owned cooperative Kuapa Kokoo. Established in 1993, this LBC subsequently became the largest Fairtrade-certified cocoa organization, and currently has about 80,000 farmer members. The managing directors of private LBCs also came in with fresh ideas around market capitalism. Because they could not compete on price, some offered other incentives – mostly to their own buyers, but a few to farmers as well. For example, the LBC Akuafo Adamfo (which means "friend of the farmer") instituted a one-for-one program, whereby farmers received one item of domestic or farming utility for every bag of cocoa they sold to the company. These were often things that only women or children use (such as cooking oil or school notebooks), which helped ensure they reached household members who have the least ability to access cocoa earnings (see chapter 5).

Domestic competition has also incentivized volume purchasing, rewarding those who buy a lot of cocoa. Some, such as district managers of high-producing areas, earn substantial incomes thanks to these incentives. Because cultural norms, especially in rural areas, dictate that those of means share with the less fortunate,[34] successful individuals may extend various supports and everyday luxuries to subordinate staff and farmers. These range from donations to funerals or sporting events (both culturally important), to communal meals or access to home entertainment. In such ways, new market entrants have helped disburse material benefits to less privileged and even vulnerable groups.

At the same time, such innovations have limited reach. Even the most philanthropic employee can only extend meals or donations so far; more importantly, LBCs face scalar constraints. Commanding about a third of the domestic market, PBC remains by far the largest cocoa buyer. Even the second largest, Akuafo Adamfo, has just half the market share of PBC.[35] Thanks to its lengthy operational history, which includes career-long personal relationships between farmers and buyers, as well as vast purchasing infrastructure and fully depreciated assets, PBC will remain, for the foreseeable future, unsurpassable. However, no LBC necessarily *wants* to surpass it. Though it sounds counter to what we are taught about capitalism, becoming too big would *cost* private LBCs profitability. The infrastructure needed to buy, store, and transport cocoa, and the logistical challenges of sourcing in rural regions, place high barriers to expansion.

I discussed this with Thomas Amoateng, a district manager for Akuafo Adamfo, who offered this analysis:

> So you asked what it takes to compete with a company like PBC. The resources for people to work with are the most important. It means expanding sheds, it means building bridges, it means employing more PCs [purchasing clerks], more vehicles to be able to move the cocoa, or bigger vehicles. If you can get those resources, if you can build the capacity – that is what you need.

Thomas turned to a purchasing clerk who had just delivered the day's cocoa, and asked how much he had bought. The purchasing clerk replied that he had purchased 1,600 kilograms. Thomas continued, "A thousand six hundred. If today, you can handle a thousand six hundred, how can you handle two thousand, two thousand five hundred? Three thousand? It's not easy. You'll have to pour cocoa on the ground for lack of resources." Private buying companies are not willing to risk costly capital expenditure to rapidly increase market share. They want only enough to stay profitable, which, at present, means not exceeding about 20 percent of domestic buying. Beyond that, profits would shrink or vanish. This means that even with a highly impactful incentive program that could woo every farmer in Ghana, at best any LBC would reach about a fifth of them, because it would not choose to grow further than that at the expense of profits.

Despite claims of liberalization's efficiencies and trickle-down benefits, in Ghana, private companies depend for their profitability on state infrastructure. With its protections and supports, the state keeps Ghana's industry productive; through PBC, it offers market access to more farmers than any other buyer. With this giant maintaining the foundation, each LBC can carve out a profitable niche. PBC of course also wants to be profitable, but the state necessarily has concerns beyond profit. The Ghanaian government still uses cocoa to demonstrate that it can serve or punish specific groups, but it also has political accountability to its more than 800,000 cocoa farmers – who earn Ghana nearly a third of its foreign revenue. It needs cocoa to maintain roads, ports, utilities, water and sanitation systems, telecommunications: in short, everything required to run a nation-state. Whether its own buying company, PBC, is profitable or not, the state cannot let the cocoa industry fail, and that is ultimately to the benefit of the private companies that have entered its market. In this cocoa context, there is a more symbiotic relationship between the state and private sector than neoliberalism would predict. Here, the Ghanaian state plays a crucial role in the functioning of the cocoa market.

Ivory Coast: full liberalization

In contrast to Ghana, every other major producer fully liberalized its domestic market, including neighboring Ivory Coast. As part of its own SAP, Ivory Coast dismantled the state cocoa board, Caisse de Stabilisation, or Caistab. Previously, Caistab had set the producer price but, from 1999, private buyers were permitted to purchase cocoa at whatever price they saw fit. The underlying neoliberal principle was that buyer and seller would share price risk: when the world market price rose, buyers would pay accordingly more and, consequently, growers would be better off than if the government had set a seasonal price. This did not take into account power differentials that favor private buyers – who often work for foreign-owned, well-capitalized firms with little interest in farmer welfare – over farmers, who have slight individual or even collective influence, may lack current price information, and may live in an area where only one buyer operates. Rather than sharing risk, farmers were merely forced to take whatever price buyers offered.

The evidence for whether full liberalization has benefited farmers is indirect and mixed. As in Ghana, by its own measure of increased exports, adjustment was a success in Ivory Coast. Production rose and beans continued to leave the country even during periods of civil unrest (indeed, cocoa has been central to Ivory Coast's conflicts; see chapters 5 and 6). Though such "conflict cocoa" is morally repugnant to many, neoliberal ideology would be more concerned with the fact that adjustment helped maintain exports regardless of political circumstance.

Another way to assess liberalization is to compare prices in Ivory Coast and Ghana. While we know Ghana's price because COCOBOD sets and publishes it, buyers in Ivory Coast do not disclose what they pay farmers in a comprehensive or routine way. However, there is a method for comparison, which is to examine the direction of smuggling between the two countries. Though I have pointed out that farmers often lack access to price information, growers along the long land border between Ivory Coast and Ghana have robust communication channels and respond quickly to price changes. Even slight price differences are magnified through the sheer volumes the two countries produce: with hundreds of thousands of metric tonnes at stake, farmers understand the potential gains if they can move cocoa to where prices are higher. Smuggling operations are organized and swift. On the Ivorian side, I have watched a seemingly endless supply of cocoa bagged into official Ghana COCOBOD sacks and prepared for immediate transport. If full liberalization did benefit farmers more than a fixed price system, we would expect cocoa to be constantly smuggled out of Ghana and into Ivory Coast. But in fact the direction has changed over time. After Ivory Coast lifted its fixed price in 1999, cocoa frequently went into Ghana, through about the mid-2000s. But by 2008, large volumes of Ghanaian cocoa were moving into Ivory Coast. This is a broad summary: there have been many sudden directional changes, which suggests that neither a fixed price nor a fully liberalized market consistently guarantees a better price for farmers.

In late 2011, the situation changed, as newly instated President Ouattara scaled back earlier SAP reforms. That the IMF and World Bank supported the changes suggests that even the institutions most loyal to neoliberalism had accepted that full liberalization was not a panacea. In January 2012, the government introduced the Conseil du Café-Cacao (CCC), a new board responsible for overseeing cocoa and coffee, replacing the lost Caistab. CCC was charged with, among other things, re-stabilizing cocoa's domestic price. Its major reforms included forward sales (that is, guaranteed purchase) of 70 to 80 percent of the next year's crop, and a guaranteed minimum price.[36] Harkening back to Nkrumah's words at his own inauguration, in Ouattara's speech announcing the minimum price, he said to cocoa farmers, "You are the true artisans of Ivory Coast's development. . . . We will finally give farmers what they deserve." Tying cocoa explicitly to state-building, Ouattara positioned himself as the leader who would reward farmers for their contribution to development.

Ivory Coast's reinstated minimum price has intensified cocoa's regional politicization. In years prior, when cocoa was smuggled into Ivory Coast, Ghana's COCOBOD frequently responded by raising its own producer price the next season. In rare cases, it even increased the price mid-season, as in 2007–8 when it made a 25 percent increase to curb smuggling. Now it responds at the start of each main harvest to Ivory Coast's minimum price, setting its own just a bit higher. For the 2015–16 season, Ouattara announced a minimum price of $1.70 per kg, and Ghana set its own at $1.76.[37] Both raised prices again for 2016–17: when Ivory Coast announced $1.88, Ghana set $1.91 a few days later.[38] The goal, of course, is to keep as much cocoa as possible within the country – and therefore taxable.

In Ivory Coast, however, forward buying and minimum price guarantees have not proven strong enough to protect farmers from more powerful forces within the industry. In early January 2017, Ivory Coast saw several days of violence that sparked fears of a return to widespread conflict. Cocoa's price rose briefly in response, but the violence subsided and price returned to its depressed level. As others had also anticipated, exporters in Ivory Coast had been counting on a price rise. When cocoa's price fell instead, they faced losses, or at least lower profits. Having agreed to purchase cocoa at one price, exporters had been planning to sell it at a higher price than actually materialized. Rather than lose out, some defaulted on contracts.[39] As cocoa piled up at Ivorian ports, there were reports that buyers were illegally paying farmers less than the guaranteed minimum price.

Contract defaults are not the norm, and these were clearly cases of private companies doing so to avoid loss of profit. This circumstance gives us insight into the power relations of cocoa's trade from this region. Ivory Coast needs to export its cocoa crop, which is foundational to its economy. Chocolate manufacturers and processors depend upon the country's vast volumes – about 40 percent of world total. While these companies benefited from the price fall that came with unexpectedly abundant supply, they still needed that supply to actually leave Ivory Coast and get to their factories. But if cocoa could be exported from Ivory Coast during the height of civil conflict, when farmers were being displaced and murdered, it would continue to do so despite a few exporter defaults. Ivory Coast's government had to resell buying contracts at lower prices and, in April 2017, accepted at least $100 million in aid from the World Bank to support its cocoa finances.[40] Even though exporting firms had defied legal contracts, cocoa still moved from Ivorian ports, to factories that added value to it, and, after that, to store shelves. This suggests a rather depressing power dynamic for an industry that ultimately depends on making people happy. Firms that occupy the very middle of the supply chain, unknown to most and virtually untouchable by consumer activism or other industry pressures, can refuse to perform their core function out of greed – and, nevertheless, cocoa will get to its ultimate destination: the mouths of chocolate lovers.

CHAPTER FIVE

Economics on the Ground

This chapter examines how cocoa trading impacts farmers in their everyday lives. The sale of cocoa does not happen in the same way across all geographical contexts, or for every farmer within the same context. Each country that grows cocoa has a seasonality and market structure that shape when and how farmers earn money. Farmers' earning potential varies depending on where they live, but also on social and political standing. To illustrate economics on the ground, this chapter translates the world market price into terms that farmers use, and then explores social and political norms that shape cocoa farming and sales in Ghana and Ivory Coast. From these examples, we can see that there is no such thing as an "average" cocoa farmer. Differences of gender, age, nationality, and ethnicity, among other social constructs, make the process of growing and selling cocoa diverse and specific, and vary the potential for earnings.

Price terms

In 2016, the organizations True Price and Sustainable Trade Initiative released a joint report entitled *The True Price of Cocoa from Ivory Coast*.[1] The admirable mission was to amass information on costs associated with cultivation, and to quantify social and environmental costs of growing, selling, and transporting cocoa in Ivory Coast. From this information, the authors sought a price figure that would reflect the comprehensive reality of what it takes to grow cocoa. They then extrapolated these findings to milk powder and sugar (which they qualified as estimations only), and added them up to find the true price of chocolate. For a conventional (that is, bearing no certification label) 100-gram milk chocolate bar with 50 percent cocoa solids, they estimated that the "true price" in a European super-market should be €2 ($2.18 at current exchange rates).[2]

But even this careful calculation, which takes into account many more farmer realities than cocoa's world market price, remains only a relatively more comprehensive assessment. It is not a "true" price in the Platonic sense, such that the number shows us an enduring, eternal reality of cocoa cultivation, even within Ivory Coast. It *is* a more accurate economic reflection of the complexity of farmers' lives than many other price estimations. But any time we put a numerical figure on cocoa, we automatically make a reductionist statement. That is, an amount denominated in a currency necessarily excludes a great deal of reality: no matter how comprehensive a set of calculations may be, there are some things that simply cannot be reduced to money. Dollars, pounds, euros – these are unable to represent back to us many qualities of life.

For example, as with all smallholder production, growing cocoa relies upon family members, friends, and neighbors whose work is not always remunerated in cash. In West Africa, neighbors frequently trade labor by helping each other break open cocoa pods, and organized work groups are common for ongoing tasks such as weeding. In addition to the trade of labor, "payment" most often comes in the form of a meal hosted by a woman of the household whose land is being worked. We can calculate the financial costs associated with those meals; the value of labor involved in preparing and serving food, cleaning up afterwards, and so

forth; and the opportunity costs of spending time on someone else's farm. But what figure do we put on the bonds of
loyalty that may be inspired by neighbor helping neighbor?
How do we account for the relationships that may develop
and endure among people of all ages, who come together
for collective work? What deductions should we make for
rivalries that arise when farmers witness their neighbors'
prolific trees when their own may be suffering? Should we
deduct for the fact that some people may have only come
together in the first place because they share an ethnic or
political affiliation, speak the same language, or went to the
same school?

The search for a "true" price is not limited to the report
cited above; it inheres in every iteration of price. Western
models of scientific reasoning valorize quantitative over
qualitative measures, and economists distance their
discipline from the *social* sciences to foster an image of
economics as "pure" science, uncomplicated by anyone's
lived reality. These reductionist systems of thought have
conditioned whole societies to *believe* numbers, to accept
them as indisputable representations of virtually any aspect
of the world in which we live. However, in this book, I take
the position that *no* price is a "true" price. Even beyond the
necessary exclusion of qualitative elements, every figure
put forward as cocoa's price comes from a data set that
is partial and limited and, moreover, serves a particular
agenda for the person or organization that publishes it. We
cannot take any price figure at face value. Rather, we must
consider the parameters within which it was derived, and
why the person calculating that price chose to work within
those specific limitations.

This chapter and the next offer several examples that
illustrate how and why each cocoa price figure, rather than
being an objective reflection of exchange value, instead tells

its own story and little more. We also need to consider the contextual factors that mediate every farmer's relationship with world market price. That is, knowing that world market price sets the terms for the international exchange of millions of metric tonnes of cocoa, what drives how much *farmers* earn from this crop? On any given day, the world market price is not necessarily the most important determinant in how much cash ends up in a farmer's hands. Other factors impact income more decisively, during the course of any sales exchange as well as over the long term.

Seasons

While many factors determine how much a farmer makes from her or his cocoa, the crop's seasonality determines *when* that money comes into the household. Unlike crops with a very sensitive harvest window, such as vanilla, cocoa pods ripen slowly and year round. However, there are typically two distinct seasons: a main crop and a less productive mid- or light crop (though in some areas there is only one season). Their timing varies across growing zones, and the difference between them is most pronounced in West Africa, where main crop (September/October through February/March) can account for up to 80 percent of a farmer's harvest.

Cocoa's seasonality relates to a critical issue of representation regarding farmer income. In the industrialized Global North, employment is typically structured as wage labor, which involves receiving pay at regular intervals. You might, for example, receive a paycheck every week or twice a month. This is a normative way of thinking about income in the Global North, but it is not the structure of cocoa income, or indeed for agriculture in general, which rarely involves long-term consistent wages. Cocoa farmers frequently hire daily laborers, especially during the busy main crop. But while these workers do receive a wage, it is neither guaranteed nor generally regulated, and its payment depends on the farmer's own cash availability. Outside of the few plantations (estimated to account for 5 to 10 percent of all cocoa production), cocoa farmers never receive a regular paycheck (and it is always possible that plantation workers are not regularly paid). The pattern of predictable pay that the word "wage" implies doesn't make sense in a cocoa farming context.

For those who own land or have use rights to sell the cocoa they grow, farmers earn cash only when they sell their crop. In Ghana, for example, this is mostly between October and March. With 80 percent of the harvest happening then, farmers earn 80 percent of their annual income in six months. During the other half of the year, they earn the remaining 20 percent from the light crop. Year round, many farmers, and particularly women, earn petty cash from diverse small businesses, including selling food, medicines, soap, clothes, and so forth. But cocoa is by and large the main income earner and its seasonality makes budgeting very challenging. If you work on a contract or freelance basis, or if your work is also seasonal, then you will comprehend the difficulty of budgeting when earning all or most of your pay during a limited period or at irregular intervals.

Because many inputs are needed at the start of the main growing season, such as fertilizer, pesticides and fungicides, boots, and cutlasses (machetes, for harvesting and breaking open pods), cocoa growers face costly expenditures at exactly the time of year when they are lowest on cash – at the end of the light crop (or no crop where there is only one season). As a result, they nearly always obtain these inputs on credit. When cash starts coming in from the main harvest, it typically goes first to repaying those debts. Only after that can a farmer spend on individual and household needs: processed foods, school fees and supplies, health care, clothing, travel, and so forth. In this way, cocoa's seasonality pushes cash toward certain expenditures and away from others. Because cultivation incurs certain costs at a specific time of year (which, in West Africa at least, is around the start of the school year), it is not possible for farmers to allocate income evenly across all productive and household (reproductive) costs, no matter how pressing any one of those may be.

Moreover, in major growing regions, the rural economy fluctuates with cocoa's seasons. In Ghana's Western region, for example, which produces more than half that country's crop, tro-tros, the local taxi-vans, are abundant and regular during the main harvest, which means both people and things – food, fuel, correspondence, sundry goods – can travel easily between rural areas and towns during those six months. The rest of the year, transportation is scarcer, and many comforts of life – including travel to see friends and family, as well as for health care – are correspondingly more difficult to access. Pregnant women will walk or be carried to a midwife during this time, medicines are less available, and news takes longer to arrive, among many other challenges. We cannot separate cocoa from these day-to-day realities – the crop's seasonality is integral to how and when farmers can meet their basic needs.

Wet versus dry beans

There are two ways that farmers sell cocoa beans: wet or dry. When a farmer sells wet beans, she or he breaks open pods, scoops out the seeds and pulp, and sells the cocoa more or less immediately. In this scenario, which is common in parts of Asia Pacific, Central and South America, and the Caribbean (though not exclusive to or universally practiced in those regions), the buyer collects beans from multiple farmers and takes them to a central facility, called a fermentary, to be fermented and dried. When a farmer sells dry beans, as is common in West Africa (though again not exclusive to there), she or he undertakes fermentation and drying, the first stages of value addition. (The exception is when farmers sell unfermented, dried beans, as in Indonesia and Uganda, among other places.) Because dry beans have been processed through two stages, they are more valuable than wet beans. In India, for example, where farmers sell both wet and dry beans, domestic purchase prices for late 2012 were 123 to 130 rupees per kg of dry beans and 28 to 33 rupees per kg of wet beans.[3] Using the exchange rate of 55 rupees to the dollar at the time, this equaled $1.05 per lb for dry beans, compared to $0.25 per lb for wet beans. To illustrate price differences between growing regions, around the same time, farmers in the Caribbean island of Grenada were earning $0.48 per lb for wet beans.

Wet beans weigh more than dry beans; 100 lb of wet cocoa yields 35 to 40 lb of dry, which is up to 60 percent weight loss. Using that percentage to adjust the India wet bean price to its dry bean equivalent gives us $0.63 per lb; farmers in India who sold wet beans earned less than half that. The difference is accounted for by the value added through fermentation and drying, and associated costs. For farmers to bring their cocoa successfully through these steps is a matter of wherewithal and skill – that is, farmers must have the necessary equipment and training to carry out fermentation and drying to the best effect. But it also depends on factors beyond a farmer's control, including the right weather conditions. Once fermented, cocoa beans are best dried quickly in the sun. But where sunny days are limited, or when rain is unpredictable, or where it is challenging to get sufficient fresh air flowing over drying beans, producing high quality fermented and dried cocoa is challenging. India is one area, along with parts of Central and East Africa, and the Caribbean, among others, where the right conditions for fermenting and drying are not always or even often present. In the India example, it is difficult to say whether farmers could be earning the higher dry cocoa price. Even if they have the necessary skills and equipment, there is no guarantee the weather will cooperate. There is always a similar set of complicating factors that influence the bean type and quality that farmers can bring to market.

Calculating price

Regardless of whether a farmer sells beans wet or dry, she or he does not receive the full world market price (which is calculated for dry beans). For example, at a world market price of $3,000 per MT, if a farmer sold one MT of dry cocoa, she or he would not receive $3,000. Rather, farmers receive what is called the farm gate price or producer price, which is the amount paid at the point of sale. It is extremely difficult, if not impossible, to accurately assess farm gate prices globally. Because virtually every major producer underwent structural adjustment in the late twentieth century, which dismantled marketing boards that set a seasonal producer price, individual buyers now often determine cocoa's farm gate price. The assumption is that buyers will pay according to the world market price: increasing the farm gate price when the world market price is high, and lowering it when the world market price falls. However, not every buying company reports on price paid. There is no global mandate to do so, which means that in many growing areas, we don't know the farm gate price. In a 2012 report, the ICCO noted that, "As a result of institutional changes and the subsequent absence of published data, it has not been possible to compile representative farm gate price series for some of the leading cocoa producing countries for recent years."[4] Ghana is the prominent exception, having maintained a remarkable degree of control over its cocoa industry even in the face of structural adjustment, including the power of COCOBOD to set the producer price. Ivory Coast recently reintroduced forward buying and a minimum price, so data from those countries are reasonably reliable (see chapter 4).

Outside of fixed price contexts, farmers may have only the option to sell cocoa to local buyers, at the prevailing local market price. Buying cocoa happens mainly in remote areas where there is little oversight of transactions, and it can be challenging for growers to assert authority at the point of sale. Farmers frequently suffer from weighing corruption, whereby fixed scales show less than the actual cocoa weight. In Sierra Leone, growers have told me that some buyers do not even permit them to look at the scales, so that farmers are forced to take the buyer's word regarding weight. In these cases, farmers are highly vulnerable to being cheated. To counter this vulnerability, farmers may come together to form a producer organization, through which they collectively manage the sale, transport, and marketing of their cocoa. Producer organizations may offer technical assistance, trainings and sensitizations, and other development programming, but a main goal is to improve the terms under which farmers sell their crop, including price.

With these different sales contexts in mind, we can translate the world market price into terms that farmers use in everyday transactions. Cocoa's world market price is quoted in metric tonnes, as are national exports and imports, total annual production and grindings, and futures contracts.

Farmers who regularly deal in large amounts of cocoa, for themselves or on behalf of a producer organization, are sensitive to the world market price per MT. Most farmers, however, even if they do sell a metric tonne (1,000 kg, or 2,205 lb) over the course of a season, deal in smaller amounts for routine transactions. When farmers have price information, they most often know the current price locally per kg or lb, and the world market price per MT is less directly relevant to their income calculations.

Because farm gate prices are not compiled and published in a central location, comparisons must draw on different sources, from research reports to newspaper articles or even documentary films. These rarely reference the same measures: some quote the wet bean price, others dry; some report price per kg, others price per lb; coming from various countries, each may report in a different currency. Thus comparisons involve calculating equivalencies across currencies and weights. After the necessary calculations, three examples from Asia and the Caribbean illustrate the dissimilar prices farmers encounter. Sometimes, factors driving price differences are evident and well understood. For example, in 2011 in Grenada, the wet bean price was $0.48 per lb for conventional cocoa. Farmers who grew organic beans, however, could sell them to the Grenada Chocolate Company cooperative for $0.74 per lb.[5] In this case, using organic methods meant farmers earned about 50 percent more for their cocoa. Since demand for organic chocolate has been rising at the consumer end, it is easy to understand why those methods command a higher price.

Other times, price differences are less easy to explain. In Grenada in 2013, the dry bean price per lb was $1.47.[6] Around the same time, India's dry bean price was $1.05 per lb, and Indonesia's was about $0.87 per lb. One reasonably certain explanation for Grenada's higher price is that farmers there grow a prized variety of flavor beans, for which they receive a premium. One evident driver of Indonesia's lower price is that farmers there do not ferment cocoa, but simply dry and sell it. Beyond that, however, we must look to many possible factors. Some farmers can undertake fermentation and drying in preferred ways, or under ideal weather conditions, which may earn them higher prices. Farmers in one context may have formed a producer organization that offers secure price terms, while others may be subject to local market prices. Infrastructure plays a role: some places have better roads and more secure warehouses than others, which impacts transportation and storage costs that buyers deduct to establish the farm gate price. Governments tax cocoa at different rates; some of these taxes may impact farmers severely, while others may not. And, in some cases, buyers pay less than they ought.

We can compare these unknowns about cocoa's price across Grenada, India, and Indonesia with the information-rich context of Ghana. There, COCOBOD sets the producer price every season. Newspapers and radio publish it widely and, from these reports, price information spreads further by word of mouth. In Ghana, all cocoa must be sold in government-issued jute sacks, which are standardized to hold 64 kg (as are cocoa bags in other places). In its price announcements, COCOBOD emphasizes the producer price per bag, and the fact that LBCs are obliged to pay it. The result is as universal price knowledge among growers as can reasonably be achieved: in my fieldwork in Ghana, I have never met a farmer who could not quote the current seasonal price per bag.

Though Ghana's producer price is well established and clear, there are a few steps involved in its calculation that are not usually explained with equal clarity. Here we must look at several other price terms. The first is all-in cost, which includes all associated costs of purchasing, storing, shipping, and marketing cocoa beans. It is the total cost of the beans, plus the costs of moving them from farms to the place where they will be processed into chocolate. These costs vary across contexts, as does the bean price, depending on quality and negotiations between buying and selling organizations. All-in costs are thus higher or lower in different places.

Sometimes buyers quote the all-in cost per MT when communicating about price. More often, they quote the FOB price. FOB stands for free on board, which is a commercial shipping term. When FOB is used, it means that the seller – in this case, cocoa farmers, or a producer organization – bears the logistical responsibility and cost of transporting goods to the port of export and loading beans onto a ship. At that point, the buyer assumes transportation and other costs, such as for insurance. Technically, FOB terms mean that farmers *own* the cocoa until the moment it is loaded on a ship, and thus bear the risks until then. But since it would not be possible to hold each farmer individually liable for her or his beans during the logistically massive process of cocoa evacuation, the FOB price is calculated for a country context or for a trade relationship between a producer organization and buyer.

From there, farmers do not receive the FOB price proportionate to the amount they sell. Instead, they receive the farm gate price, which can reflect other deductions or additions. If, for example, the farmer belongs to a producer organization that has a certification, the farm gate price may reflect a premium for that certification. Sometimes, a government body sets a guide price to indicate how much farmers should receive. Other times, a powerful buyer in a local market can de facto "set" the farm gate price. While farm gate prices broadly reflect FOB, they are not set as a strict proportion of it.

Let's return to Ghana for a closer look at the farm gate price. The government takes the FOB price for Ghana and makes a further deduction – taxes – to establish the producer price. With its tax revenues, Ghana's government supports a vast cocoa infrastructure and an extensive quality control system. While these benefits have not always been regular or sustained, COCOBOD has supplied growers with agricultural training, inputs, seedlings, and mass spraying to control pests and diseases, among other things. It employs graders who travel the country, performing rigorous quality tests and classifying beans. Thanks to this oversight and support (and of course thanks to the farmers for their superior husbandry), Ghana produces the best bulk beans in the world. Its cocoa trades on the futures market for a premium, which COCOBOD passes onto farmers in the form of a "bonus" to the producer price. In 2016–17, it added 5 Ghanaian cedis (GH₵), bringing the total amount paid to GH₵475 per bag. This equaled $122.50, or $0.87 per lb.

$0.87 per lb is the same price that Indonesian cocoa farmers received for dry beans four years prior, in 2012. That same year, Ghana's price per lb was $0.80, or 8 percent less than what Indonesian farmers received. In the study citing Indonesia's $0.87 price, 37 percent of farmers reported participating in certification schemes, which may have added a premium to the price paid.[7] But even with that certification rate, Ghana's producer price ought still to have been higher. Due to inferior husbandry methods and lack of expertise combating disease and pests, Indonesian cocoa is considered low quality. Most is sold unfermented and can only be used in conjunction with fermented beans from elsewhere to make cocoa products. In contrast to

Ghana's high quality and price premium, Indonesian cocoa is discounted on the futures market. That farmers in Ghana received a lower price than farmers selling inferior cocoa in Indonesia reveals that they bear a heavy tax burden.

This political reality is not lost upon growers. Ebenezer Tandoh, the farmer from Kramokrom who explained that he could do nothing with his beans apart from sell them, recognized that by growing more cocoa than any other domestic region, farmers in his area "fetch the government a lot of income." He then described what I have also witnessed throughout Ghana's rural areas: unreliable electricity, insufficient sanitation facilities, poor schools, and inadequate housing. The problem was not that farmers weren't producing enough cocoa to fund improvement of all those things – it was that the government was not reinvesting cocoa taxes in farming communities. Ebenezer told me, "The world market price is not given to the farmers, we are given some producer price. The taxes in it will go to the government." I asked what the government would do with that money. Ebenezer replied, "According to the government, they use that money for development. That is what I know. But you don't see development happening here."

These are just some of the complexities of price. Political actors, national policies, and other influences subtract from and, less frequently, add to the world market price before it reaches growers. Country and region, extent of market liberalization, accessibility of certification schemes, availability of information, variations in husbandry, wherewithal to undertake fermentation and drying, cocoa politics in other countries – all these, among other factors, influence how much any farmer earns for her or his labor. Cocoa sales are thus never strictly economic; each growing country has a specific *political* economy, which always operates in relation to political economies elsewhere.

Socioeconomics on the ground: Ghana

Within any national context, not every farmer experiences the political economy of cocoa in the same way. While overall prices paid to farmers *are* low, relative gain and suffering depend on social factors. Statistics often cite average productivity or income, but few individuals match the description of an "average" cocoa farmer. We must also look at ranges and, even more importantly, social norms that shape farmer livelihood.

In my 2013 research in Ghana,[8] the range of bags farmers reported selling per season was 1 to 85. At 2016–17 prices, farmers who produced the least cocoa (1 bag) earned $122.50 for a season's work and those who grew the most (85 bags) earned $10,413. Women reported mean sales of 8 bags, which brought in $980, and men 23, which earned them $2,817.50. To make a comparison, the 2015 gross national income (GNI) per capita in the UK was $43,700:[9] more than 44 times higher than the average amount women in Ghana earned selling cocoa in my survey, and more than 15 times higher than men's average earnings.

A common question I get when making such comparisons is, "But isn't the cost of living so much less in Ghana?" That is, aren't Ghanaian farmers' earnings enough for a reasonable standard of living, because things are cheaper there? The answer is yes and no: everyday goods are cheaper in Ghana, but not so much that an annual income of $122.50 or even $10,413 makes for a comfortable living. If we take women's average production of 8 bags at 2016–17 prices, that annual income of $980 works out to $2.68 per day (remember that most earnings come into a household over six months, and farmers are unlikely to portion them out into daily amounts for a year). For comparison, store-bought bread is about $0.85, and a dozen eggs from a supermarket in Accra cost $2.86 – already more than a day's average allocation for expenditure.

Even this estimate paints a rosier picture for cocoa farmers than most, and it is crucial to note that neither my research findings nor my example of women's average cocoa earnings are necessarily representative of Ghana as a whole. In 2014, a reporter for US broadcaster NBC interviewed a farmer whose income was similar to what I found, about $3 per day,[10] and noted that this placed the farmer in Ghana's "lower middle class." Other estimates are lower. *Cocoa Barometer 2015* reported an average cocoa income in Ghana of just $0.84 per day – a figure that appears to take into account farming costs, and thus may give a more accurate idea of what farmers can spend on their personal lives.[11] A study commissioned by Cadbury in 2008 that surveyed 217 farmers in the Ashanti, Western, and Eastern regions found an average cocoa income for all household members of $0.42.[12] Comparing these figures shows that, as with price, there are many ways of reporting income, each of which offers only partial insight. For example, if we think through the mathematics, we would expect that last figure to be lower than the others, because it represents cocoa earnings divided by number of people in a household. But confronting that number – $0.42 – reveals a reality of farming income that my own $2.68 per day figure may not. A $2.68 daily expenditure allocation is low. When measured against the cost of goods in Ghana, we can see that it buys little. But the $0.42 number forces us to recognize that farmers seldom, if ever, retain the whole of their earnings for themselves. When divided among everyone who depends upon it, cocoa farming means a life of material poverty.

But there is more to the story of income. While the

Cadbury report figure of $0.42 per day asks us to recognize that farming income must be shared in a household, by itself it cannot tell us how readily everyone in that household can access their share. For this, we need contextualized analyses of socioeconomics. Even income estimates that disaggregate by gender do not show how deeply social norms structure farmers' livelihoods. Across West Africa, social relations of gender shape what is and is not possible for any farmer. Historically, married women and men own land as individuals and keep separate budgets. There are, of course, families that combine income but, in general, husbands and wives control their own earnings. Women and men are also responsible for different kinds of expenditure. Men make payments on housing and (often) school fees; they also pay for cash crop inputs, such as fertilizers and farm equipment. Women are entrusted with food, health care, (sometimes) school fees and supplies, and clothes – collectively known as reproductive responsibilities, as they maintain reproduction of the family. Again, there are many exceptions, whereby men contribute to, for example, health care. But this is the typical structure of married household budgeting.

Agricultural goods are also gendered, such that either men or women are responsible for them and control proceeds from their sale. Export crops are almost always male, whereas subsistence goods are usually female. When large areas of West African farmland previously designated for subsistence cultivation were allocated to export crop production, in colonial and postcolonial periods, the shift had a sustained negative impact on women. Increasing the amount of land devoted to export crops meant men controlled more farming income, and women lost means to meet reproductive responsibilities.[13]

Gender patterns in cocoa farming have disproportionately negative effects on women; that is, labor and remuneration structures do not balance out in the advantages and disadvantages they confer upon women and men. Cocoa farming involves many steps, from clearing a field, to planting, pruning, weeding, spraying, harvesting, breaking open pods, fermenting, and drying beans. While both women and men perform most of these steps, some are more strictly gendered than others, such that either women are preferred for them or only men can do them. As anthropologist Ester Boserup argued, when agriculture "modernizes" – for example, when cash crop production expands, or a new technology is introduced – women's labor tends to be devalued and they lose power. This can be over proceeds, land, or a particular stage in the growing process. For example, in cocoa farming in Ghana, one of the most valued activities is mechanical application of pesticides and herbicides, because this tends to noticeably increase yields. Men do the spraying of trees, almost exclusively. Steps that women perform, such as planting and harvest, are comparatively devalued, because these do not impact yields as noticeably in the short term. (This is despite the fact that integrated agroforestry approaches to cocoa cultivation do place high value on these steps and see them as vital to sustainability.) Planting and harvest are also done by hand, whereas spraying involves a machine, which makes the former seem less "modern."

In fieldwork, whenever I have asked why only men spray herbicides and pesticides, men *universally* respond that women cannot carry the machinery. Indeed, when I have queried the rationale behind women's exclusion from any task, responses typically presume their inferior physical capabilities.[14] For example, women do not work as graders for Ghana's COCOBOD, a socially respected wage labor job. The reason, men have often claimed to me, is that women cannot walk the long distances between cocoa depots. (A colleague reported hearing another explanation: women cannot drive motorbikes to make these journeys.) Since women in Ghana routinely walk long distances (by one estimate, 6 kilometers, or 3.7 miles) every day to carry water and firewood to their homes, usually on their heads, it hardly seems likely that they could not walk to a grading station – or, indeed, carry a spraying machine, whose weight, unlike that of a bucket of water (a US gallon of which weighs more than 8 lb), is disbursed by a backpack suspended from the shoulders. Because the overt rationale of physical capability does not seem to hold true, these responses must reflect instead the social construction of gender: a specific belief system about which behaviors are appropriate for women and men.

This is not a uniformly oppressive system. In fact, while gender norms constrain women in cocoa farming more than they help them, proscriptions on performing certain tasks offer women some relief from already heavy daily labor. In addition to productive endeavors, women are responsible for providing food, water, fuel, and health care, as well as cleaning and supervising children, not only for their households (which may include extended family members) but also for others in the community (bachelor neighbors, for example). They do this in an environment that offers little infrastructure – for example, running water or hygienic sanitation systems. In this regard, women may welcome exclusion from particular farming tasks, or from jobs such as grading cocoa that would require them to walk even longer distances than they already do to fulfill domestic responsibilities.[15] However, that does not make these exclusions any less impactful on their earnings.

Economically, it matters whether women do the spraying or work as graders. Women, even when married, typically retain control over any land they own and earnings from it. But if social norms dictate that only men can do a particular farming step, such as clearing a field, heavy weeding, or spraying, then a woman must *find a man* to do that work. Women may ask husbands, sons, brothers, uncles, or nephews, who often willingly comply, but many do not, or they may cheat the woman out of earnings or labor. If a woman has migrated from elsewhere, she may have no family members nearby to call upon. When a woman cannot find a man to do the work, she must hire someone, spending meager earnings on laborers. Of course, farmers everywhere – including men in Ghana – hire laborers, and both women and men do so for many reasons, including simply having too much to do on their own. The point is that gender norms compel women's labor dependency in specific ways, and diminish their power to control production of a crucial crop. Gender norms regarding women's "lesser" physical capabilities also make them less desirable as tenants, who make up a large proportion of farmers. Recent research by UK-based charity Twin showed that just 7 percent of tenants in surveyed areas in Ghana were women.[16] Tenancy not only provides a source of income and food, it is a key route, outside of inheritance, to becoming a landowner.

None of this is necessarily specific to West Africa. Social norms that devalue women's labor are common the world over, and the constraints that women face in Ghana would likely look familiar to farmers elsewhere. Nor, of course, are women a homogenous group. Gender norms are most constraining when a woman also suffers from oppressions based on age, ethnicity, migrant status, and marriage status, among others. Elderly widows, for example, are often relatively powerless. Even when they own land, they face more extreme forms of dependency to grow and sell cocoa. In contrast, the first wife of a prosperous farmer, whether landowner or tenant, may enjoy preferential treatment in her community and have the social status to command certain men to work on her behalf.

For all women, gender constraints are most potent at the point of sale. Across West Africa, women predominate in markets for subsistence goods, but men control cash crop sales. While women sometimes sell cocoa, social norms usually demand that, at the point of cash exchange, only men are involved. Women typically enlist men to sell their cocoa; if a woman is married, this is usually her husband, but if she is unmarried or her husband is unable to help, she must find another man to act on her behalf. Thus at the moment when farm labor comes to fruition, cash typically goes into men's hands.

Several challenges arise from this. Because many cocoa farmers in Ghana are illiterate and innumerate, they don't often keep written sales records. When a man brings a woman her earnings, she has no proof that she is receiving the correct amount. This is problematic both when a woman sells cocoa from her own land, and when a wife combines her cocoa with that of her husband. In the latter case, the woman cannot tell who earned how much. Furthermore, because men control cocoa earnings, they have immediate access to the largest source of household cash. Faced with pressing debts accumulated at the start of the growing season, as well as responsibility for large domestic expenditures, it is very common for men to use cocoa earnings to meet such needs before distributing money to women and children. Those with a tendency to vice spend the cash on alcohol, cigarettes, gambling, and mistresses – behaviors I have observed in my fieldwork. Indeed, that their husbands spend cocoa earnings on mistresses and alcohol ranked among the top complaints for women I have interviewed.

As a result, women – married or not – are frequently unable to pay for those areas of life for which they are responsible, including food and health care.

There are exceptions. Women are not universally barred from selling or buying cocoa. Two LBCs in Ghana, Kuapa Kokoo and Akuafo Adamfo, encourage women's participation at the point of sale. Kuapa Kokoo holds democratic elections to the position of recorder, the person responsible for buying cocoa on behalf of the cooperative. Because the cooperative has gender quotas for elected roles, women sometimes (though not often) hold this position. Through educational programs, Kuapa Kokoo encourages farmers to keep written sales accounts and husbands and wives to share this information. Akuafo Adamfo, which hires cocoa buyers (called, in this case, purchasing clerks), encourages women to apply, though few are literate enough for the work. In cases where women do act as buyers, their presence can help level out gender inequity in a crucial moment of trade. Overall, however, the situation remains one of gender disparity, to the detriment of women who farm cocoa.

Sociopolitics on the ground: Ivory Coast

Ivory Coast presents a political contrast to neighboring Ghana. Where the latter is peaceful and enjoys stable democratic governance, the former has suffered from violent conflict and political turmoil for more than a decade. While cocoa was exported throughout Ivorian conflicts, on-the-ground reality for many farmers has involved fear, displacement, and murder. As the analytical lens of gender reveals certain everyday realities for farmers in Ghana, in Ivory Coast, ethnicity – or, more accurately, nationality – is a crucial analytical lens.

In the 1960s, Ivory Coast began to expand cocoa production, increasing exports almost fourfold over two decades. By the late 1970s, Ivory Coast had overtaken Ghana to claim the number one cocoa spot, a position it has held ever since. Extraordinary growth in cocoa and coffee exports, and corresponding national economic development, are referred to as the Ivorian miracle. Migrant farmers were at the foundation of this achievement.

As Matthew Mitchell has documented on the basis of fieldwork in Ivory Coast, there has always been migration in West Africa (indeed, throughout sub-Saharan Africa), but the rationale and goals of migration have changed.[17] In the precolonial period, people migrated for environmental reasons and food security, and there was a general ethos of inclusiveness. During the colonial period, from the late 1800s through the mid-1900s, imperial powers encouraged migration to areas dedicated to agriculture and mining; the vast agricultural transformation of the time was thanks in large part to the arrival of people from elsewhere in West Africa. After Ivory Coast achieved independence from France in 1960, the welcome to migrants continued for about a decade, owing to pan-Africanist ideals and visions of continental political economic solidarity. The first post-independence president, Félix Houphouët-Boigny (himself a cocoa farmer), promoted migration, most notably through a 1963 policy that gave land rights "to those who make it productive."[18] This policy was to become a catalyst for conflict.

Migrant farmers made Ivory Coast prosperous to the point that journalist Órla Ryan notes its largest city, Abidjan, was known as the "Paris of Africa."[19] Yet in the 1980s, when the debt crisis took hold across developing nations, Ivory Coast began to struggle financially. Eventually, as did most postcolonial states, Ivory Coast turned to the World

Bank and IMF to take further loans to service its debt. In accordance with the neoliberal ideology that was by then influential, Ivory Coast underwent SAPs that dramatically scaled back the role of the state, including dismantling its cocoa oversight board, Caistab, and undercutting social supports. In a country now facing "belt-tightening" and economic stagnation, political sentiment toward migrants changed. Instead of being heralded as bringers of the economic miracle, migrants were targeted as the source of all Ivory Coast's problems.

As both the US and Europe have experienced in recent years, migrants are the perennial scapegoats for any population that is feeling hard done by. Ivory Coast migrants were also unfairly singled out as the cause of economic decline. In particular, the large numbers of migrants from Burkina Faso, an arid Sahelian country to the north, who had been particularly successful cocoa farmers, suffered; although, as Mitchell points out, all migrants – even those who came from other parts of Ivory Coast – were subject to threats and violence. In contrast to the former sentiment of inclusion, now migrants were identified as Other. Colloquially referred to as "strangers," migrants began to be displaced from land they had farmed, sometimes for generations.

By the early 1990s, national discourse, particularly between presidential candidates, had shifted, and notions of civil rights began to be tied to the idea of *ivoirité*, or true Ivory Coast-ness (a term first used by then-president Henri Konan Bédié). This identity was linked to the land, expressed as an idea of belonging to the soil. As with the so-called "one-drop" rule in the US, whereby individuals with any African-American ancestry at all were classified racially as black, connecting identity to "the soil" was intentionally obscure and fluid. How long does a person have to work the land to be considered "of the soil?" How could anyone prove such a link? Literally anyone could be targeted for not belonging to the land. The notion of *ivoirité*, as with the current discourse of hatred toward Mexicans and Muslims in the US, was a scapegoat mechanism whereby people feeling left out of economic prosperity targeted a perceived threatening group. In this way, nationality became central to on-the-ground realities of cocoa farming in Ivory Coast, especially as about a quarter of the country's population was estimated to be migrants.

The key political event came in 1998, when President Bédié instituted the Rural Land Law that effectively reversed Houphouët-Boigny's 1963 policy.[20] Instead of awarding land rights to those who worked it, this time the law *prevented* foreigners from owning land. Individuals now needed to demonstrate Ivorian citizenship to prove land rights. Across the country, the law added fuel to the fire of anti-migrant sentiment. It is important to note that while Houphouët-Boigny's earlier policy had granted "ownership" to whoever was farming the land, the codification and enforcement of land rights in West Africa are not the same as in Europe or North America. Rather than possessing a printed legal document that specifies boundaries, landowners often rely on verbal agreements made in a customary manner. Boundaries are frequently demarcated by particular trees or bushes, which only someone with personal knowledge could identify. Land rights are taken seriously, but they are also easy to contest. Local chiefs usually have the final say and may grant rights only to retract them later; when a new chief assumes power, he may withdraw previously granted rights. Even when documentation exists, ownership disputes may become cases of "he said, she said," and whichever party is in favor with the arbiter typically wins. In conjunction with the general climate of hostility toward migrants, the 1998 Land Law meant that many migrants' claims to land were contested by people presenting themselves as true Ivorians. Because it was only too easy to accuse someone of being a stranger, indigenous farmers also suffered; virtually no one in Ivory Coast was safe from land appropriation or threats of it.

Whether one was labeled as a "false" or "true" Ivorian meant the difference between displacement and remaining at home, and sometimes between life and death. Mitchell cites estimates that by mid-2011, during a contested presidential election (see chapter 4), more than 320,000 people were displaced within Ivory Coast and 200,000 had fled the country,[21] mainly to Liberia. Most of these, he notes, were from cocoa regions. While a relatively peaceful period followed resolution of the presidential dispute, with Alassane Ouattara assuming office in 2011, tensions remain high. Mitchell's 2012 fieldwork documents widespread fear in the cocoa regions, among both migrants and indigenous people. One new source of tension is that to protect their land, migrants have been hiring *dozos* – hunters-turned-mercenaries – who have been responsible for attacks. While Ouattara has declared that migrants are welcome in Ivory Coast, his presidential pronouncements cannot overnight change realities on the ground.

Given these wide-ranging, everyday challenges for cocoa farmers, whose precarious livelihoods supply a luxury good for millions, we must ask what can be done to ameliorate these circumstances. The next chapter examines programs that aim to increase support for farmers, and promote justice across the industry.

CHAPTER SIX

Trade Justice

Guilt-free pleasure?

Free trade, Fairtrade, direct trade: these terms frame conversations about how to make life better for cocoa farmers. The word that is common to all of them is "trade." Globalization, though often portrayed as having "left out" poor agricultural producers in the Global South, actually integrates them quite fully through trade. Cocoa farmers in Belize, Papua New Guinea, or Tanzania participate just as much in globalization as chocolate shoppers in New York City, London, or Tokyo: they grow a good that is processed or eaten on every continent (yes, including Antarctica).[1]

As a result, when initiatives seek justice for farmers, the vehicle is typically trade. It is less common to encounter suggestions that concerned individuals or companies engage in philanthropy (benevolent charity), volunteerism (offering unpaid time, experience, or skills), or abstinence (restraining consumption). While many do some or even all of these, they are usually not considered viable large-scale alternatives to trade. Radical options – for example, a comprehensive switch to growing subsistence food crops – might be beneficial to farmers over the long term, but they are not always realistic or necessarily preferable. Were cocoa husbandry to cease, consumers would lose an enjoyable food and farmers would lose a major livelihood option with few viable alternatives immediately available.

But cocoa trade *is* in need of reform. Contemporary trade relations have structural roots in colonialism, a goal of which was to secure raw materials for European factories to make luxuries like chocolate (see chapter 3). In this scenario, cocoa was *supposed* to be cheap, and trade structures have not changed so much that cocoa farming has become lucrative. Breaking down the price of a chocolate bar into portions captured by different actors shows that farmers are among the most poorly compensated for their efforts. Make Chocolate Fair! created an illustration of a 100-gram bar, retailing at €0.79 ($0.86), divided into estimated proportions that go to different actors along the supply chain.[2] The image makes it clear that the largest share of the retail price – 44 percent – goes to retailers themselves. Chocolate manufacturers take the next largest share, at 35 percent, and 6.6 percent goes to cocoa farmers (in the 1980s, their share was estimated at 16 percent). People who transport and trade cocoa collectively take the smallest share: just 2 percent. From these figures, it is clear that the people whose labor is at the foundation of the supply chain earn only a small proportion of chocolate's retail value. Moreover, that retail value – €0.79 – is absurdly low, considering the effort required to grow cocoa and make chocolate (see chapter 3). While activists rightly point to corporate profitability as a gross imbalance in the value chain, consumers also *benefit* from trade injustice. We are used to paying only a little for chocolate and balk at higher prices for what has long been an affordable luxury. This is not to say that shoppers are consciously acting unethically when buying low-priced chocolate. Rather, that low price is part of what sustains an unjust system in which consumers play a role.

Yet even if every shopper agreed to start paying $10 per bar, it would not necessarily improve farmers' lives.

When a chocolate bar costs that much, it is reasonable to assume that a higher proportion of its price is still going to retail overhead, packaging (very expensive and hardly ever discussed), marketing, distribution, freight, and manufacturing than to farmers. This is all especially true for small makers, who necessarily incur higher production costs proportionate to their output. There is a tendency to represent small-batch, craft chocolate makers as inherently more ethical than those operating at an industrial scale, but the fact is that making 100 bars is more expensive in virtually every way than making 10,000. Certainly, some craft makers do pay premium prices for beans, but it is a mistake to assume that if a bar costs $10, nine of those must be going to a farmer. Chances are they are not.

Even more importantly, cocoa's low price is only one among many sustained challenges that farmers face (see chapter 5). Oppressions based on gender, age, nationality, and ethnicity, among others, persist regardless of how much anyone pays for cocoa *or* chocolate. When cocoa's world market price rose to its highest level in thirty years during the 2011 conflict in Ivory Coast, migrant farmers there were still getting driven off their land and murdered.

Thus when considering trade justice, it is important to keep two things in mind: one, no model is a panacea, able to turn on its head an entrenched global system that benefits mainly large companies and chocolate shoppers. Two, selling cocoa is but one aspect of a farmer's life. If my salary doubled, many of my financial concerns would ease, but it wouldn't change my gender, race, class, sexuality, nationality, or any other aspect of me. It is the same for farmers: even with improved trade terms, those who enjoy a position of power usually continue to do so, while the oppressed remain so. Trade alone cannot change a political or social system. When asked to name their justice priorities, for example, Indonesian cocoa farmers included land tenure security and a fair, transparent legal system – issues that no trade initiative can really address.[3] This chapter cannot, therefore, offer a list of "guilt-free" bars, which guarantee that every contributing farmer lives in sustained material comfort, personal safety, and emotional fulfillment. Such chocolate does not exist.

With those qualifiers, I address four trade models: free trade, Fairtrade, organic, and direct trade. If it is important to you to buy chocolate from a company that is doing its best, according to its vision and mission, to make a positive contribution to cocoa farmers' lives, then this chapter will help you understand the possibilities.

Unfree labor

Before analyzing trade justice initiatives, it is important to understand an egregious element of the industry: that of "unfree labor," including child labor, on cocoa farms. The use of unfree labor has a long history in cocoa. From demands for cocoa tribute by ruling Aztec kings, to enforced production by Spanish colonists in the Americas, through the importation of African slaves in South America and the Caribbean (see chapter 2), the violent exploitation of humans has been a recurrent feature of cocoa production. The issue returned to public attention largely thanks to Brian Woods and Kate Blewett's film *Slavery: A Global Investigation* in 2000 (inspired by Kevin Bales's book, *Disposable People: New Slavery in the Global Economy*),[4] which interviewed child laborers who had been abused and imprisoned on a cocoa farm, and included recreated scenes of torture and a boy telling chocolate lovers that they were "eating [his] flesh." A host of initiatives to eradicate child labor followed, from the US Harkin–Engel Protocol in the early 2000s to a 2016 class action lawsuit against Nestlé and Cargill on behalf of alleged child slaves.[5]

Studies published by the International Institute of Tropical Agriculture (IITA) and Tulane University have estimated unfree child labor across West Africa at less than 2 percent.[6] In the 2002 IITA report, an estimated 0.94 percent of farmers surveyed in Ivory Coast and an estimated 1.1 percent in Nigeria (0 percent in Ghana and Cameroon) reported using permanent, salaried child workers.[7] Among those children who were non-family cocoa farm workers, an intermediary had been involved in recruiting an estimated 41 percent in Ivory Coast, and an estimated 29 percent in Nigeria. In Ivory Coast, most of the children had come from Burkina Faso, and about a quarter from elsewhere in Ivory Coast. None reported that their parents had received a payment in exchange for them, all had left home voluntarily, and all understood before leaving home that they were going to work in cocoa. Again in Ivory Coast, 29 percent said that they would not be allowed to leave the cocoa farms where they were employed if they wanted to do so, and an additional 11 percent said they lacked the funds to leave. While these figures give us insight into the extent of recruited child labor in Ivory Coast and Nigeria in particular, as of 2002, we must read them as we do every other figure in this book: as partial, unfixed, and resulting from the specific parameters of the research that arrived at them. It is possible that, at the time, actual labor rates were higher, or lower, than farmers or children reported. If child labor rates fluctuate with cocoa's world market price, which is at a ten-year low, they may rise. They may also fluctuate with socioeconomic cycles as yet unstudied. I offer these findings not as established, permanent fact, but as a starting point for understanding the scale and scope of unfree child labor in West Africa's major growing countries.

Partly because this issue resonates so forcefully with chocolate consumers (see chapter 1), a great many resources – more than $15 million by one estimate[8] – have been directed at initiatives to reduce or eradicate child labor. To date, there is little evidence that these have been effectual. At the consumer end, some suggestions have been impracticable. For example, US Senator Tom Harkin (Democratic party, Iowa state) advocated that companies charge more for chocolate and spend the money eradicating child labor, suggesting that just pennies per bar would do it.[9] The Senator's career-long commitment to children's education led him to co-witness what ultimately became the Harkin–Engel Protocol, along with Congressional Representative Eliot Engel (Democratic party, New York state). Engel had proposed that the 2002 Agricultural Appropriations Bill assign funds for a "slave free" label requirement for chocolate. However, industry players paid former Senator Bob Dole to lobby against the bill, with the result that it did not pass in the Senate. Chocolate companies agreed instead to "set out time-bound steps to eliminate the worst forms of child labor and forced labor from all cocoa farms worldwide by July 2005"[10] – a promise that relevant organizations, including the industry group World Cocoa Foundation, have since admitted was unachievable. A report by the International Labor Rights Forum (ILRF) in 2008 concluded that this voluntary agreement had achieved little, if anything.

Targeting multinational chocolate companies alone, however, is too limited. Their tremendous scale and purchasing power mean they *can* exert influence on the governments of cocoa producing countries to reduce labor abuses, and activists should continue to put pressure on them. But by themselves they cannot change what happens at farm level. Moreover, chocolate companies are not the only parties that benefit from or sustain egregious labor practices. We can include everyone from traders, to retailers, to people who eat chocolate. Farmers' livelihoods are precarious in part because shoppers in wealthy countries enjoy cheap chocolate. Those livelihoods are threatened further by climate change and the relentless depletion of forests to make everything from lumber to toothpicks. These are not "far away" problems, localized and specific to West Africa or any other growing region. They are *global* problems, because cocoa production and chocolate consumption are inextricably linked. In fact, all commodity production and consumption are bound together, economically, environmentally, and even morally. Behaviors of excess and overconsumption in the Global North play no small role in the enduring poverty and suffering of *all* farmers.

There is no simple solution. There is only complexity, and correspondingly complex pathways to change. First, we must understand that labor abuses happen not because farmers are evil, but because generations of desperation have the ability to normalize egregious practices. Moreover, there is nothing *inherent* about cocoa farming that causes unfree labor. Children in West Africa work in harmful conditions across many industries, including urban ones. The work is often gendered: girls frequently labor as domestic servants, and some in sex work. Boys take dangerous jobs in transportation. Both hawk goods in hazardous positions on the streets. Singling out cocoa as a sector that uniquely endangers children exposes the cognitive dissonance that results from wanting to eat chocolate – a luxury associated with romance, holidays, and happiness – while not wanting to harm children. Because consumers in the Global North do not benefit from child labor in, say, domestic service in Ghana, chances are they do not experience the same personal conflict upon learning that such exploitation is happening. But were an initiative to make it impossible for children to grow cocoa, there is every chance they would be absorbed into other industries where conditions are as likely to be harmful.

We must also reject the simplistic assertion that labor is easily categorized into "free" and "unfree." Media accounts suggest there is a clearly delineated group of people who have been forcibly removed from home and made to work without pay indefinitely, much as slavery happened historically in the US. As Stephanie Barrientos and her colleagues have pointed out, a more practicable way of addressing the issue is to examine the various *ways* that laborers can be unfree, and the circumstances that deny people labor freedom.[11] In West Africa, the most important constraint is lack of livelihood opportunities in the Sahel, the starting point for regional migration. This arid zone bordering the Sahara Desert is much poorer than the fertile areas that lie toward the Atlantic coast. Faced with the certainty that remaining home offers only grim prospects, adults and children migrate south to comparatively richer agricultural regions. In contrast to Western media portrayals of cocoa farming as an evil lure, for Sahelian migrants, cocoa has long represented an opportunity for *advancement*. It is a strange luxury for journalists, activists, and other concerned people to be able to denounce the whole West African cocoa industry, of which they generally have no firsthand knowledge, particularly when that industry provides an indulgence that many of them personally cherish. Condemning cocoa farming or even its potential abuses is much less of an option for people living in dire poverty in the Sahel. Instead, those people may look to cocoa farming with hope.

Nevertheless, while migrants choose to leave in search of work and are not usually captured or stolen, the decision to leave is itself forced, driven by lack of opportunity.[12] And the "chosen" labor *can* be coercive and harmful. Again, this is not unique to cocoa farming or to West Africa. We can consider, for example, the young men and women in Europe and North America born into poor communities who join the armed forces. These young people may see no other path to stable employment and voluntarily enter a labor situation that could involve grievous injury or death. Migrants in West Africa, however, are typically vulnerable in ways that armed forces servicewomen and servicemen are not. Migrants often cannot access state services, may not speak local languages, and may lack the wherewithal to make the return journey. All of these are especially true for children.

From this, we can understand why certain initiatives will not eliminate unfree labor. The oft-suggested idea of charging more for chocolate to ease farmer poverty reverses typical cause and effect, whereby higher cocoa prices drive higher chocolate prices.[13] Moreover, when cocoa's price does rise, it makes migration to farming regions even more attractive. Arresting people who promise migrants work only to exploit them, or who transport children from home, targets individuals when the problem is systemic. Buying only cocoa from outside West Africa would do more harm than good, endangering as it would the millions of honest, hardworking people who depend on cocoa to feed and shelter themselves.

But nor does the situation's complexity mean we must throw up our hands and leave child laborers to suffer. Instead, the clear imperative is to use systematic evidence from cocoa regions that demonstrates the nature of unfree labor and successful methods for addressing it. Here, Business and Sustainability professor Amanda Berlan's findings have been enlightening.[14] Her work clarifies, first, that children's labor can make important contributions to a family while not being harmful. Over fifteen months of fieldwork in Ghana, Berlan's child-friendly ethnographic research found no instances of children who had been brought from elsewhere, and for many their work was safe and valued. Crucially, Berlan reveals that, as in most places, parents and school were the two biggest influences on whether and how children engaged in farm work. Adults considered whether farm work had potential value for a child, including developing a professional skill set, relative to available schooling. Children thought too about how they might benefit. Whether food was more likely to be available on the farm or at school was one consideration; another was whether teachers would be present at school and, if so, whether they were likely to use corporal punishment. From Berlan's research, it is clear that adults *and* children weigh many factors regarding health, safety, and livelihood when deciding whether children work on a cocoa farm.

These findings describe children whose work was not characterized as harmful. Berlan also studied labor that posed a physical or emotional threat to children. Berlan found that household dynamics, particularly the break-up of families through divorce, primarily determined whether a child undertook hazardous labor. That is, what goes on in children's homes is the most important factor. Divorce in the Ashanti region, where Berlan conducted fieldwork, is not uncommon. Women can file as well as men, and historically women have used divorce as a strategy for regaining control over household resources when these were not fairly shared by husbands.[15] Though gender hierarchies often work against women in such suits, sometimes the women succeed. Berlan's research shows that when a household breaks up due to divorce, children typically remain with their mothers. Because women often do not personally sell cocoa, it is difficult for them to access enough cash to meet large expenses, such as for housing and school fees (see chapter 5). When, as Berlan found to be often the case, ex-husbands refused to pay for children's upkeep, children faced little choice but to undertake paid labor. Children involved in harmful farming practices most often came from households where there was no male head. In the absence of the major income earner – a man – children were effectively forced into labor.

It is clear that social relations of gender are a main driver of the worst forms of child labor. Though gender is often discounted as subordinate to the "real" issues, in fact it is central. No effort to eradicate harmful child labor in cocoa farming will succeed without addressing relationships between husbands and wives, men and women, parents and children. In the too-common scenario of a household losing its main income earner or a father refusing to pay for children's upkeep, women and children must appeal to the state. Berlan documented women and children who visited Ghana's Social Welfare Department and success-fully argued their cases, winning maintenance to which they were entitled from fathers. She also suggests that the Women and Juvenile Unit of the Police Force protects chil-dren's labor rights and safety in farm work. These are not institutions that consumers can directly impact by purchas-ing a particular chocolate bar, or even that a multinational company can influence through cocoa purchases. The important actor is the nation-state – here, the Ghanaian government – which can continue to resource these organi-zations and enforce laws that protect women and children.

Beyond individual scholars, the International Cocoa Initiative (ICI) has commissioned studies and issued reports that shed light on issues of child labor in Ghana and Ivory Coast. The ICI has worked in both countries since 2002 to bring together cocoa industry and civil society groups – in dialogue with farming communities and government participants – to "[promote] child protection in cocoa-growing communities."[16] Crucially, and in contrast to the idea that chocolate companies alone can resolve this issue, the ICI works within the frameworks already provided by national policies in those two countries to guide its research and actions. In its current program cycle, from 2015 to 2020, the ICI is engaging in 360 cocoa growing communities to establish child labor monitoring systems, and continuing advocacy at the national level.[17] Though it is challenging to see how, logistically, any study or initiative could put forth a comprehensive assessment and action plan around child labor for the five million growers across the cocoa industry, this type of bottom-up, community-engaged research and programming may provide a basis from which to respond to child labor injustices more widely.

Free trade

Discussions of trade justice often involve the terms "free trade" and "fair trade." This can be confusing, as both sound positive. But they mean different things. Free trade is trade on neoliberal terms, which hold that governments should play no role in the market. Recently, politicians in the US and Europe have called for increased protectionism, including promises to keep or return jobs to their countries. These statements can sound novel because, for several decades, neoliberal ideology has pushed governments to eliminate or reduce trade regulation, through regional agreements (such as the North American Free Trade Agreement – NAFTA – or the EU single market) and by adopting the free trade mandates of the WTO. But the fact is that powerful nation-states have *always* protected their economies. They do this by imposing tariffs and quotas, subsidizing industries (especially agriculture), and enforcing measures that maintain the interests of corporate constituents. Truly free trade could only happen when no government imposed any of those protections.

For cocoa, free trade describes beans bought and sold according to the world market price, which is set by futures trading. But futures markets are far from accessible to all. Because few people conduct futures trading, working with information and financial supports that are not generally available, we may ask whether this price setting is truly "free." The futures market is, however, freer from government involvement than the cocoa trade was historically. In the early colonial period, European countries placed tariffs on cocoa imports to protect themselves and their colonies, making cocoa's price an extension of nationalism. Once those tariffs eased, the same countries tended to place high import taxes on chocolate, making the chocolate trade far from free (see chapter 3). Neoliberalism demanded that these tariffs ease, as they did with, for example, the establishment of AGOA in the US. AGOA encouraged African countries to export chocolate (among other goods) by eliminating US import tariffs. Economically, this was a freer arrangement, since it took away the tax that African manufacturers would pay to send chocolate to the US. However, to be eligible for AGOA terms, African countries had to demonstrate "improvements" in enforcing the rule of law, protecting human rights, and respecting labor standards.[18] While desirable, these prerequisites mean that African governments must govern in a way the US deems appropriate before they can export chocolate duty-free. Politically, then, this trade is not free. The reality is that no global trade truly is. Even when some protectionist measures are eliminated, other regulations or trade clauses (like AGOA) typically continue to favor powerful countries, and to reflect their political priorities.

Fairtrade

Fairtrade is a dedicated label overseen by the not-for-profit organization Fairtrade International (formerly Fairtrade Labelling Organizations International, or FLO). It offers what is called third party certification, meaning that an unrelated entity – not the cocoa producer, not the chocolate company – confirms that everyone is complying with agreed-upon trade terms. This is conveyed to shoppers through a label on chocolate packaging. Other third party certification schemes for trade justice include Fair for Life,[19] Fair Trade USA,[20] and Utz,[21] but Fairtrade is the largest of all labeling efforts in this category. Its voluntary certification program offers independent verification for about a dozen agricultural goods, several composite products (containing multiple ingredients), and manufactured goods.[22] Thanks to its scale, Fairtrade has achieved notable successes, including raising consumer awareness of trade injustice, and advocating for dialogue and action within the cocoa industry. Its model also leaves itself open to critique, and I address both Fairtrade's successes and its limitations.

Trade terms: benefits and critiques
Fairtrade International is an intermediary between *labeling organizations* and *producer organizations*. Labeling organizations certify that chocolate companies comply with Fairtrade price terms, and that producer organizations comply with Fairtrade producer terms. Fairtrade requires that at least half a producer organization's members be smallholders, using mainly family labor and not hiring

year-round workers. Producers must practice environmentally sustainable farming, and adhere to International
Labour Organization conventions for hired workers,
including freedom from discrimination and forced labor,
freedom of collective bargaining, and protecting children
from the worst forms of child labor. Producers must elect a
governing board using democratic methods.

To cover the costs of auditing to ensure compliance with
those requirements, producer organizations pay an annual
certification fee. The revelation that producer organizations
must pay a fee to be certified is often startling to consumers,
and rightly so. If the reason-for-being of Fairtrade is that
growers are not receiving just remuneration for their labor,
then a fee must add to existing financial challenges at origins. Another way of dealing with this would be to pass the
cost on to consumers, who benefit from audits through the
reassurance that producers are complying with terms that
they care about. That Fairtrade does not currently opt for
this route raises questions. Increasing bar prices to capture
certification costs from consumers could make Fairtrade
chocolate less competitive than non-certified bars, which
might cause Fairtrade's market share to plateau or fall.
But if certification fees are a burden to producer organizations, and if shoppers are paying an unjustly low price for
conventional chocolate, then requiring consumers to cover
certification costs would be a way of enacting justice along
the supply chain.

Of course, there is a financial component to Fairtrade
that benefits producer organizations. In return for complying with its terms, producer organizations receive a
Fairtrade Minimum Price and Fairtrade Premium. The
Fairtrade Minimum Price is what economists call a price
floor, which means buyers must pay at least that amount.
Since January 2011, the Fairtrade Minimum Price for cocoa

has been $2,000 per MT. If the cocoa world market price (or any set price, as in Ghana) is higher than $2,000, then producer organizations receive that higher price. This element of Fairtrade deserves both appreciation and critique. On the one hand, when a price floor is put into place, it protects producer organizations from market volatility, at least below the level of the floor. Neoliberal policies have eroded the capacity of governments in the Global South to offer subsidies, price floors, or other protections to farmers. Countries that export cocoa were not rich to begin with, and they have suffered from the combined effects of structural adjustment, pressure from the WTO, and bilateral agreements to "free up" trade. While preaching an ideology of free trade, powerful nation-states routinely protect their own domestic agriculture, including with price floors. By setting a Minimum Price, Fairtrade suggests that agricultural producers in the Global South deserve protection too.

On the other hand, the Fairtrade cocoa price floor is low. The role of the Minimum Price is to "ensure that producers receive prices that cover their average costs of sustainable production."[23] But the same Minimum Price applies to all certified cocoa producer organizations (at the time of writing, 129 organizations in nineteen countries), which necessarily have different production costs, and it is unclear which was the basis for the Minimum Price. If it was, as the definition implies, an *average* for all of them, then some producer organizations will have higher costs than the Minimum Price can meet. Moreover, Fairtrade International has only raised the cocoa Minimum Price once, in 2011, when it revised up to $2,000 from $1,600 per MT. Between the time of that upward revision and April 2017, the monthly average price of New York futures never fell below $2,000 (although at the time of writing, the daily trading price was below that, so the monthly average may dip below $2,000). This means certified cocoa producer organizations never had to rely on the Fairtrade Minimum. Lack of regular revision means, at the very least, that the Fairtrade Minimum is not keeping up with inflation rates (which, again, vary across countries). But its stagnation also raises questions about its relevance. If the price floor never goes into effect, then we must ask whether the Fairtrade Minimum is only an ideological statement, and not a benefit of practical importance to producer organizations.

The other element, the Fairtrade Premium, is an amount paid over and above the cocoa price. Since January 2011, the Fairtrade Premium for cocoa has been $200 per MT (when it increased from $150). Premium monies go to "a communal fund for workers and farmers to use to improve their social, economic and environmental conditions."[24] Because producer organizations must be democratically organized, farmers get a say in how this money is spent. Sometimes, members (or their elected representatives) decide to use Premium funds to make direct payments to growers; in 2014, nearly a third of Premium funds for cocoa were used in that way. Most of the time, though, governing boards vote to invest Premium funds into a project, equipment, or infrastructure that will benefit a village or the organization as a whole, including mobile health units and ambulances, boreholes and water pumps, spraying machinery, cutlasses, vehicles, buildings, and organic certification, among others.[25]

When chocolate bears the Fairtrade label – a blue, green, and black shape that looks like a yin yang – it means that the cocoa and all other ingredients in the bar were traded in accordance with the terms I just described. This is the case so long as Fairtrade certification is available (for example, there is no certification for salt, so a Fairtrade salted chocolate bar would include salt that is conventionally traded). Fairtrade International reports that 1.2 percent of cocoa is traded under its auspices.[26] Seeking to expand opportunities for sales, the organization introduced the Fairtrade Cocoa Program. This allows products to include only certified cocoa, while other ingredients – for example, sugar in a chocolate bar – can be conventionally traded. The program's terms also permit companies to buy just a portion of their cocoa as Fairtrade. While the program website celebrates its potential to extend Fairtrade benefits to more growers, we can challenge this method of scaling up. It may be difficult for consumers to differentiate between Fairtrade and Fairtrade Cocoa Program labels, as they use similar imagery, but the programs are different. The former certifies that all ingredients in a chocolate bar have been traded under Fairtrade terms, and the latter only the cocoa, or even just a portion of it. While this may indeed bring Fairtrade benefits to more farmers, it does not have the same integrated ethical commitment that the original label carried.

But we must credit Fairtrade with a different kind of achievement, which has been to promote awareness that people living comfortably in the Global North enjoy luxuries like chocolate thanks to the labor of materially poor farmers. Though the process had begun at least a century earlier, the increasing trend in North America and Europe in the 1950s was toward supermarket-ization of food provision, which dramatically increases the geographical, emotional, and even visceral distance between shoppers and the origins of what they eat and drink. The norm of growing, processing, and preparing food within an intimate circle of family members and community providers diminished, and food became easily accessible, cheap, and abundant regardless of season. It became ordinary to shop for foods not local to temperate climates – including cocoa, avocados, bananas, and coffee. As these products seemed to magically appear on supermarket shelves, it became difficult to see that *all* foods come from actual places on the map, where real people work hard to produce them.

In the 1990s, media attention to textiles, cut flowers, and certain food crops began to suggest that all this cheap abundance was based on a foundation of suffering. Fairtrade International expanded that momentum, and further critiqued the dehumanization of supply chains by offering stories about the real individuals behind global food supply. By the early 2000s, consumers and companies were responding with greater urgency, and trade justice inched closer to becoming an expected norm, rather than an exceptional circumstance for a fortunate few. We can trace current discussions of justice – even the Polity Resources series – to the spotlight that Fairtrade shone on poverty's links to trade. And by offering a way to take action – buying certain products instead of others – Fairtrade reinforced a notion of accountability for consumers. Fairtrade International has communicated its notion of trade justice widely. The organization has regional associations for producers in Africa, Asia, and Latin America (including the Caribbean), which include seventy-four countries and 1.5 million farmers and non-farm workers.[27] In 2014, there were 129 certified cocoa producer groups with 179,800 members, who farmed 434,300 hectares and produced 218,000 MT of cocoa, of which 32.4 percent was sold under Fairtrade terms. These are notable achievements. There is no question that Fairtrade has raised awareness of trade injustice, and introduced a mechanism by which growers have been able to enjoy material benefits that conventional trade would not have brought them. But given the scale of trade injustice, it is also important that Fairtrade, as the leading and largest labeling organization, keep its terms as robust, responsive, and progressive as possible.

Industry impacts

Fairtrade's achievements of scale have influenced the largest industry players to change the way they communicate about sourcing. From offering little or no information to consumers about supply chains, the Big Five have begun to participate in conversations about certification, and to purchase Fairtrade cocoa. In 2009, Cadbury began sourcing Fairtrade certified cocoa for Dairy Milk.[28] In 2013, Nestlé began offering certain KitKat products with Fairtrade certification.[29] The next year, Ferrero made a three-year commitment to purchase 20,000 MT of Fairtrade certified cocoa from Ivory Coast.[30] In 2015, Mars began selling Mars Bars with Fairtrade certified cocoa in the UK and Ireland.[31]

At the same time as they joined the conversation about trade justice, however, these companies introduced even more ambiguity into the landscape of its practice. Hershey, for example, claims to purchase about a third of its cocoa from certified sustainable sources, but discloses neither the proportions that come from each of its three certifiers (Fairtrade, Utz, and Rainforest Alliance), nor the impacts of these purchases on growers.[32] In late 2016, Cadbury relinquished Fairtrade certification in favor of an in-house sustainability guarantee by Cocoa Life. Its parent company Mondelēz plans to certify all Cadbury products in the UK and Ireland under Cocoa Life terms. While the UK Fairtrade Foundation declared its support for the move, citing the potential to offer trade benefits to more farmers,[33] switching from third party certification to an internal scheme opens the door to *decreased* transparency around trade terms.

When a certification scheme is internal to a company, it

is more difficult to assess whether terms are rigorous and consistently applied. The only option is to take the company's word that they are. Moreover, as internal (or even third party) certification schemes proliferate, it is harder for shoppers to compare and contrast them. While a growing number of consumers appear interested in purchasing certified products, few have the wherewithal in their busy lives to sit down and assess the details of every scheme, assuming they all offer comparable information. If one certification program is weaker than another, that will not be evident to a shopper facing an array of labels that all claim to support a similar goal. And because *any* label will set a chocolate bar apart from those that do not have one, there is no real imperative to make the trade terms behind those labels as strong as possible. Instead, knowing that any claim to sustainability or trade justice adds value to a chocolate bar, companies may end up in a race to the bottom, offering only the weakest certification standards.

For producers, it is unclear whether internal certification schemes will retain the capacity-building potential of Fairtrade (or, indeed, any of its elements). To become certified Fairtrade, cocoa producer organizations must be democratically organized, and build and maintain robust internal systems of governance and communication. The potential for farmers to organize around buying, selling, and marketing their cocoa – a central feature of the Fairtrade model – is less clear in internal schemes such as Cocoa Life. The infrastructure required to communicate and enforce standards of production in rural regions is extensive, and it is unclear how Cocoa Life will develop such an infrastructure. And while the amounts that multinational companies invest into cocoa sound impressive, we must ask whether any amount will have a lasting impact if the farmers have few or no organizational channels through which to express their own priorities and intentions to maintain the future of their crop.

Kuapa Kokoo

While Fairtrade requires adhering to a common set of trade terms, certified producer organizations may structure programming to reflect members' specific socioeconomic and cultural challenges. Among these, Kuapa Kokoo took an early lead in addressing social relations that shape farmers' lives, particularly gender. Too often, trade discussions marginalize gender, considering it irrelevant to market exchanges. This reflects a false assumption that people can set their gender aside to focus on the "real" issues. Kuapa Kokoo, however, has made gender a central analytic and basis for action since the cooperative was founded in 1994.

Kuapa Kokoo has gender quotas for elected representation at community and district levels of governance. While there is no quota for Kuapa Kokoo's national governance bodies, thanks to those that exist at lower levels, as well as programs that encourage women to take leadership positions, there is higher than usual representation of women at the national level. In fact, the two most recent presidents of Kuapa Kokoo Farmers Union have been women. Though women often lack the literacy and numeracy skills to undertake the role, they are encouraged to serve as purchasing clerks (which the cooperative calls "recorders"), who are charged with buying cocoa on behalf of Kuapa Kokoo. The cooperative has organized more than 1,300 members and their spouses into about fifty consciousness-raising women's groups across Ghana's growing regions. Programs range from income diversification projects to structured discussions around household gender inequities. For example, because women typically do not participate at the point of sale, and because it is common for husbands to keep any written records of sales to themselves, women are often unsure how much cocoa they or their husbands have sold. Training emphasizes the importance of record keeping and information sharing, providing women with crucial leverage in household budget negotiations.

Research that I led in 2013 showed women's lack of literacy to be a critical area of disempowerment: just 23 percent of women farmers reported being able to read Ghana's lingua franca, Twi, compared to 68 percent of men. Inability to read made it harder for women to manage cocoa sales, but also to navigate everyday life. In response, in collaboration with Ghana's Non-Formal Education Division and with the support of Divine Chocolate, Kuapa Kokoo organized women's literacy programs in Twi and English. The results have been positive, and they can also be heartrending. After literacy training, one woman related how much easier it was for her to take trips from the farm into town, because she could read the destination signs on buses and find the correct one to take her home.[34] Perhaps because it is often taken for granted by people who grew up in the Global North, literacy scarcely appears in trade justice discussions. But as this example illustrates, learning to read can be profoundly empowering for farmers.

By making gender central, Kuapa Kokoo has sent a message that it recognizes women's everyday challenges and directs resources to ameliorate these. This has had a positive impact on its business, by helping to grow membership and therefore cocoa purchases. In recent surveys, when women were asked what had motivated them to join the cooperative, members responded that it was because they heard Kuapa Kokoo did good things for women.[35] At the other end of the commodity chain, Divine Chocolate has led the industry in making women farmers visible to chocolate shoppers. An advertising campaign that ran in major magazines and newspapers in the early to mid-2000s in the UK featured women members of Kuapa Kokoo. The images challenged stereotypical Western representations of black African women, by showing fashionable farmers in command of their desires, holding pieces of chocolate.[36] In an industry that has often rendered cocoa farmers invisible, the Divine ads made clear the incontrovertible fact that women, negotiating complicated, multifaceted lives, are behind every bar of chocolate.

Organic

A different approach to justice involves organic certification, which puts concerns for human and environmental health at the forefront. Like Fairtrade, organic involves a third party certifier whose label appears on the chocolate bar. The UK company Whole Earth Foods was an early leader in organic chocolate, launching the Green & Black's brand in 1991 (acquired by Cadbury in 2005, now Mondelēz). Since the 2000s, several companies have made organic chocolate more widely available in the US, notably Dagoba Organic Chocolate (established 2001, acquired by Hershey Company in 2006), Taza Chocolate (established 2005), and Theo Chocolate (established 2006). As demand rises, production of organic cocoa has increased, although it remains a fraction of global totals. Due to the reluctance of many buyers to publish prices or even volumes purchased, the precise amount of organic cocoa today is unknown, and estimates disagree. In 2009, the Tropical Commodity Coalition put organic cocoa at 20,000 MT, or about 0.6 percent of total production.[37] Five years later, Dutch organic processor Crown of Holland estimated that 1.5 percent of all cocoa was certified organic,[38] but the ICCO estimated less than 0.5 percent.[39] What is certain is that countries in Latin America and the Caribbean export the most certified organic cocoa. Peru and the Dominican Republic are the leading exporters, and smaller numbers of farmers grow certified organic cocoa for export in Asia Pacific and Africa.

As with Fairtrade, organic certification requires producer groups to pay a fee and provide documentation that individual growers are complying with organic standards. There are various certifications, which mostly originated in mature chocolate markets. That is, farmer groups did not decide what organic certification should entail; it was a top-down endeavor. Consumers often interpret organic to mean chemical-free, but this is not necessarily the case. Cocoa is susceptible to many threats, and farmers may welcome the opportunity to use pesticides and fungicides to keep trees healthy and yields high. Organic certification *may* permit them to use synthetic chemicals to combat disease and pests, or to fertilize trees, when no alternative is feasible. However, in general, organic regulations emphasize holistic crop management and discourage the use of synthetic materials. Certification schemes prioritize the integrated health of the ecosystem, which includes cocoa trees, farmers that manage them, coexisting flora and fauna, and, at the other end of the supply chain, chocolate consumers.

In exchange for managing cocoa farms according to these priorities, producer groups with organic certification receive a price premium. Between half and two-thirds of all organic cocoa is also certified Fairtrade, and Fairtrade International offers a fixed premium of $200 per MT for organic. That is, a Fairtrade producer group whose farmers grow organic certified cocoa receives an additional $200 per MT as premium. (Fairtrade also sets a higher Minimum Price for organic cocoa, of $2,300 per MT, compared to the $2,000 per MT price floor for non-organic cocoa.) Organic cocoa that is not certified Fairtrade also receives a premium, though in these cases the premium is not fixed by any organization, and is estimated at $100 to $300 per MT.[40] Direct trade arrangements may also demonstrate commitment to an organic ethos, whether or not a producer group has certification.

Transitioning to organic can be financially challenging. Typically, if a farmer has used synthetic inputs to maintain tree health, when she or he stops using them, yields decrease. It usually takes three years, during which time a farmer cannot use inputs prohibited by the certification scheme, before cocoa can be labeled organic and receive a price premium. So, during those three years, farmers may lose out twice: once from lower yields that result from loss of synthetic inputs, and again because they are not yet receiving an organic premium. Even after certification, farmers may not make enough from organic premiums to meet the costs of production. Crown of Holland estimates that organic methods can yield less than half the output of conventional methods. This is a dramatic difference for a crop whose farmers live within tight margins. Organic certification thus can put growers into a challenging situation. If a farmer wants to practice farming methods that are healthy for herself, the surrounding environment, and chocolate consumers, she may have to sacrifice yields and, at least for a time, earning potential.

Direct trade

Some companies have gone a different route to third party labeling, and practice direct trade. Few chocolate companies as of 2017 have made this choice, so it is difficult to make generalizations about the model. However, those that currently do use it are explicit that the goals are to source fine flavor beans (see chapter 7), for which they will pay a higher price than bulk beans command, and to direct resources over the long term to assist producer organizations in maintaining their output of high quality cocoa. The direct trade pioneer for chocolate is Taza, based in Somerville, Massachusetts. When Taza Chocolate opened in 2005, its founders had visited the Dominican Republic, purchased cocoa from La Red Guaconejo cooperative, airshipped it to Boston, and brought it to the factory to make chocolate. This approach was financially direct: Taza paid La Red for the beans and no middlemen were involved. By shrinking a commodity chain that is often far-flung, no step of the trade exchange, from farm to factory, was unknown or untraceable to Taza's founders.

Since then, Taza has expanded its Dominican Republic sources to include ÖKO Caribe and Finca Elvesia, and initiated trade relationships with producer groups across Central and South America. In Bolivia, Taza co-founded cocoa processor and exporter Alto Beni Cacao Company. Taza was the first US company to source organic cocoa in Haiti, from processor and exporter PISA (Produits des Iles SA). Together with the organization Uncommon Cacao, run by Emily Stone, Taza helped establish Maya Mountain Cacao in Belize and invested in Cacao Verapaz in Guatemala, offering growers technical assistance and premium market linkages. As this list illustrates, Taza invests money, time, and human resources to improve quality, facilitate market access, and develop organizational infrastructure for farmers. In several cases, these investments have offered fresh marketing opportunities for growers. For example, chocolate consumers in the UK may have already been familiar with Belize as a source of superior cocoa, as Green & Black's made its first bar, the Fairtrade and organic certified Maya Gold, using cocoa from that country. Maya Mountain Cacao, however, helped bring Belize into wider renown in the US, where it has become a prized origin for craft chocolate makers.[41]

Taza has also taken steps to clarify and codify its trade model by publishing five direct trade commitments: (1) "Develop direct relationships with cacao farmers," including visiting farmer groups at least once per year; (2) "Pay a price premium to cacao producers," of at least $500 per MT above the world market price, with a price floor of $2,800; (3) "Source the highest quality cacao beans," defined as 85 percent or higher fermentation rate and 7 percent or less moisture; (4) "Require USDA [United States Department of Agriculture] certified organic cacao"; and (5) "Publish an annual transparency report."[42] For each, Taza explains its verification method: dated invoices of prices agreed with farmer groups, flight receipts for staff traveling to origins, quality assessment records, and so forth. Quality Certification Services, a USDA organic certifier, verifies that Taza meets its commitments each year. An important point is that both Taza and its producer organizations have responsibilities to fulfill, in maintaining relationships and verifying quality. According to its reports, Taza bears the costs of its direct trade commitments, including travel and reportage.

The fifth commitment, to publishing an annual transparency report, was a first for the chocolate industry. Taza introduced its *Direct Trade Transparency Report* in 2011 and, as of 2016, just one other company had followed suit: Dandelion Chocolate in San Francisco, whose *Sourcing Report* launched in 2014. Before the Taza report, craft chocolate companies often claimed to be paying up to several times the world market price for cocoa, and linked this to improved circumstances for farmers. However, no company published prices until Taza began that practice. In addition to price data, both Taza and Dandelion reports describe each producer group and the company's relationship with it. Both indicate which staff members visited producer organizations and when. In an industry that has been historically secretive, this offers remarkable transparency.

It is clear from their reports that Taza and Dandelion are paying producer organizations more than the world market price – in most cases, much more. The amount Taza paid to Maya Mountain Cacao and Cacao Verapaz was more than 75 percent higher than the 2015 average New York futures price (see table 6.1). While Taza publishes FOB prices, meaning the price producer organizations receive to bring cocoa to the port of export, Dandelion's report lists all-in costs (see chapter 5), which reflect costs beyond those included in FOB. Because we do not know these additional costs for Dandelion's transactions, we cannot compare the prices the two companies paid. We can note that the lowest all-in cost for Dandelion in 2014 was for Ambanja producer organization in Madagascar, at $4,900 per MT, and the highest was for San Juan Estate in Trinidad, at $7,440.

Table 6.1 Taza Chocolate FOB prices, 2015	
Cocoa organization (country)	FOB price paid per MT
Finca Elvesia (Dominican Republic)	$3,346
ÖKO Caribe (Dominican Republic)	$3,406
PISA (Haiti)	$3,560
Alto Beni Cacao Co. (Bolivia)	$5,200
Maya Mountain Cacao (Belize)	$5,600
Cacao Verapaz (Guatemala)	$5,600
2015 average New York futures price	$3,135

Source: Paid prices are from Taza's 2015 *Transparency Report*; I calculated average world market price using ICCO price data.

It is also important to note that, for both companies, the prices indicate the amount paid per MT to producer organizations. The figures do not indicate farm gate price, meaning how much any farmer received when she or he sold cocoa. As discussed in chapter 5, farm gate prices are not well publicized, so this is not a price obscurity unique to direct trade. However, there is a possibility that consumers misinterpret the impact of these prices on growers. Of course, there are ways that a high price paid to producer organizations can benefit farmers. But absent such information, we simply do not know – and cannot assume. While direct trade schemes are raising the transparency bar for the industry, there is room to raise it even higher, and to publish information about farm gate prices.

Comparative justice

When speaking about the cocoa industry, I am often asked which chocolate is the "best" for helping farmers. In response, I share the point made at the start of this chapter: no program is a cure-all. The benefits of any one program are not necessarily replicable elsewhere, with a different group of farmers, or at a different time, which means that no model should become a universal goal. While we can critique the models and demand more rigor from all of them, comparing outcomes is an exercise in circular thinking. Fairtrade and direct trade were never intended to operate on the same scale, and each offers benefits that the other cannot. Direct trade focuses on small-scale arrangements for the exchange of high-value flavor beans. Fairtrade offers a model for improving trade terms and developing organizational capacity and governing infrastructure for any producer group that wants to participate, regardless of the type of beans they grow. In 2015, Taza paid higher FOB prices to producer organizations than the

Fairtrade Minimum Price and Premium could match. In total, those producer organizations involved 1,876 farmers. In 2014, 179,800 farmers sold to Fairtrade certified producer groups. Which is more important, in a global industry that pays a pittance to millions: a program that extends its benefits to many growers, or one that pays producer organizations a higher price? These outcomes are not comparable, and the most farmers benefit when both succeed in their mission.

Rather than ranking them, we must assess the trade justice accomplishments of any initiative or company against its own vision. Chocolate shoppers have a responsibility here too, to examine their own priorities for justice and seek companies that best align with those. Most importantly, by envisioning multiple ways of bringing greater remuneration and material benefit to growers, Fairtrade and direct trade have both widened the scope of what it means to treat farmers equitably. By working on several fronts, they are pushing the industry as a whole to respond.

CHAPTER SEVEN

Governing Quality

Cocoa quality is partly a matter of physical attributes. A bean's strain or type, genetic composition, health (including degree of disease and pest impact), color, size, shape, and weight all contribute to quality classification. But classifying quality also has political elements, which have varied over time and across contexts, and according to the priorities of the people and entities that are influential in the industry. One way of understanding the politics of quality is to consider that its governance – how quality is measured, valued, and enforced, and by whom – is not a bottom-up endeavor. As with organic, farmers did not decide what qualifies as superior or inferior cocoa, and they do not instruct chocolate companies or consumers how to think about their crop. Rather, scientists, historians, non-governmental organizations, state regulatory bodies, commodity exchanges, chocolate companies, and even consumers in the Global North qualify, quantify, and regulate cocoa quality. This chapter examines both aspects of cocoa quality: its material properties and its politicization. In the conclusion of this chapter and in chapter 8, I address organizations and projects dedicated to bringing cocoa growers more fully into quality discussions, and to providing them with information and tools to effectively communicate about quality in trade exchanges.

Classifying cocoa

In Aztec markets, cocoa was categorized by its place of origin, with prices corresponding to the relative fineness of beans. Once Cortez and his conquistadores began to mingle with the Aztecs, Europeans learned to differentiate cocoa types too. But when the Industrial Revolution changed cocoa from a relatively inaccessible drink to a mass-produced cheap sweet, mentions of origins gradually disappeared at the consumer end. Historian Emma Robertson has traced how raced and gendered imagery from origins figured into Rowntree and Cadbury advertising through about the 1960s.[1] But as consumer markets in Europe and the US matured, depictions of the relationship between cocoa origins and chocolate diminished, and marketing strategies relied more upon a brand identity tied to features of the finished product. As a few companies came to predominate, the *idea* of chocolate was reduced to the flavors, shapes, inclusions, or even packaging of popular brands (see chapter 4). At the chocolate consumer end of the value chain, quality shifted from being an aspect of cocoa, with some bean types known and prized, to inhering in a consistent taste experience. At the farm level, this meant that quality became less about bean type or local distinction, and more about whether the cocoa was clear of rubbish, dried to a suitable moisture level, free of mold, and so forth – in short, whether it was factory-ready. As big companies rolled out bar after consistent bar, they built brand loyalty. To achieve identically flavored chocolates, they also needed to de-emphasize cocoa's natural variety.

Bulk and flavor
When manufacturers blend cocoa beans of varying origins and types, flavor and color differences between them are

diluted and muted. The result is that a Hershey's bar always tastes like a Hershey's bar, instead of like the flavor of any particular cocoa harvest used to make it. This process of blending – or bulking – beans gave rise to the broadest classification of cocoa quality: bulk and flavor beans. Bulk beans are the foundation of the global chocolate industry and today grow mainly in West Africa.

Ghana, as usual in the cocoa world, is an exception. Since at least one Big Five company – Cadbury – historically maintained its reputation and scale using beans from Ghana, and because Ghana has, even after structural adjustment, retained a high level of regulatory control over its cocoa industry, the country produces the highest quality bulk beans on the market. Thanks in large part to a long history of COCOBOD oversight and support, Ghanaian farmers have cultivated cocoa for a consistent flavor, which many consumers in Europe and North America have come to know as *chocolate's* flavor. For example, the US company TCHO, which labels each chocolate with its predominant flavor characteristic, uses "chocolatey" to describe its Ghana bars.[2]

Flavor beans, on the other hand, are those that are perceived to have a rare or prized flavor profile. They are not generally blended with other types of beans, and are used by chocolate makers and confectioners – historically in Western Europe, Japan, and parts of Latin America, and increasingly today in the US – that want to offer a distinct flavor experience. Many criteria are used to assess flavor beans, including genetic material, acidity, fermentation and drying levels, color, disease and pest degradation, mold – and, of course, flavor. The ICCO provides the following list of tasting notes that can qualify a bean as flavor rather than bulk: fruit, floral, herbal, wood, nut, caramel, and "rich and balanced chocolate bases."[3] The definition admits to being both scientific, with quantifiable aspects such as acidity levels, and subjective. I may prefer the taste of "rich and balanced chocolate," and you may prefer a combination of nut and caramel, and if we were both on the panel that determined whether a bean qualified as flavor, we might be challenged by these differences in preference. It is not an exact or objective science.

But the motivations and process behind flavor classification also bear scrutiny, which reveals the politics of this classification. The ICCO estimates that, a century ago, flavor beans accounted for 40 to 50 percent of all cocoa; today, the estimate is around 5 percent. The two major exporters of flavor beans are Ecuador (75 percent of exports) and Trinidad and Tobago (100 percent of exports). In 2015, the ICCO Ad Hoc Panel on Fine or Flavour Cocoa recommended classifying all cocoa exports from the following countries as flavor: Bolivia, Costa Rica, Dominica, Grenada, Madagascar, Mexico, Nicaragua, and Saint Lucia. It further recommended classifying 90 to 95 percent of exports from Colombia, Venezuela, Jamaica, and Papua New Guinea as flavor.[4] The only West African origin to achieve flavor status recommendation was São Tomé and Príncipe, for 35 percent of exports. No other West African country appeared on the list of those being considered. This is not because West African cocoa lacks good flavor. As I have discussed, Ghana's flavor has long been prized, and there are pockets of rare beans across the region that deserve recognition. ICCO recommendations for flavor classifications are not based on inherently superior quality.

Instead, this is a political process, driven at least in part by the influential companies whose representatives sit on the panel – including Nestlé and Valrhona among chocolate makers, and Olam and Daarnhouwer among cocoa trading houses.[5] Only governments can put forward an application for flavor status, though chocolate companies and producer organizations can offer support and evidence. An application must describe the country's cocoa history and crop genetics, but it has a better chance of succeeding if it can demonstrate that the country is already exporting cocoa at a price premium. This may diminish the role of objective quality measures and subjective flavor aspects, and instead prioritize origins that already have industry support. If a company has the means to invest in a particular producer organization and to purchase its cocoa at higher than world market price, that can help an application succeed. But because flavor designation applies to countries, not producer organizations, it can make *all* cocoa from that country seem more precious – which in turn enhances the original investment. Flavor designation thus perpetuates a system whereby producers that already receive attention and investment achieve even higher status and visibility. At present, with few exceptions, these are in Central and South America, and the Caribbean. Producer countries in Africa and Asia Pacific are celebrated much less frequently as flavor bean origins.

Criollo, Forastero, Trinitario
Beyond bulk and flavor, the industry has long depended on another classification system with three categories: Criollo, Forastero, and Trinitario. Recent advances in cocoa genetics have shown these to be rough geohistorical classifications with little botanical basis. However, the terms still appear frequently, including as a marketing tool on chocolate bar packaging. The classifications as I describe them are messy, because use of these terms has varied across contexts and over time. The point to remember is that even though they are often portrayed as distinct and hierarchical, these cocoa categories are more geopolitical

inventions than they are reflections of naturally occurring bean types.

Criollo has long been the most prized of the three. Criollo trees, which are presumed to be indigenous to northern South America, over time became the prominent cocoa type among the Maya and Aztecs. After European conquest, population loss and disease devastated Mesoamerican production of Criollo cocoa. Spanish (and, later, Portuguese) colonists began replacing those lost cocoa stocks with trees they had discovered growing elsewhere in South America. Because it looked and tasted different to well-known Criollo varieties, this unfamiliar cocoa earned the name Forastero, often translated as "strange" or "foreign."[6] The two categories have also been used, confusingly, beyond Central and South America. *Any* cocoa local to a particular area might be called Criollo, and *any* unfamiliar cocoa labeled Forastero. Forastero-named strains are generally of the Amelonado type, which is hardier and more productive than Criollo. The cocoa trees that moved to West Africa were often of the Forastero variety, leading to a common association between that region and Forastero cocoa. The third category in this long-used system is Trinitario, which is the name for any hybrid of Criollo and Forastero types. Trinitario beans are named after the island of Trinidad in the Caribbean, because it was there that the first hybridization between Venezuelan Criollo and Amelonado from other parts of South America is believed to have taken place. The result was a new type of cocoa that was more resistant to disease than Criollo, but had a better flavor profile than typical Forastero.

New classification systems
Recently, geneticists, botanists, and historians who study cocoa have revealed a far greater diversity than the above

classification system allows. Beyond the trinity of Criollo, Forastero, and Trinitario, cocoa in fact has many varieties – called strains, varietals, types, or cultivars – that have distinct characteristics. In 2008, Juan C. Motamayor, along with colleagues at the USDA and collaborators in France, Brazil, and Ecuador, published results of a study of over 1,000 samples of *Theobroma cacao*.[7] The authors identified ten genetic clusters, with thirty-six sub-clusters of five or more specimens. This means there are at least ten variations of *Theobroma cacao* that are genetically related enough to group them together. Of Criollo–Forastero–Trinitario, the authors found enough evidence to retain only Criollo as a genetic group. Among cocoas that had been labeled Forastero and Trinitario, they found too much variation to keep these as useful categories. Instead, they offered ten genetic classifications, named for their geographical area or the name traditionally used for the type of cocoa most represented in that group: Marañon, Curaray, Criollo, Iquitos, Nanay, Contamana, Amelonado, Purús, Nacional, and Guiana. They then mapped these categories to the source locations of specimens in Central and South America. On their map, Criollo appears almost exclusively in Central America, and the others in northern South America (with the one exception of Amelonado in Central America).

As revolutionary as it was for cocoa genetics, the new classification has not, as yet, had wide exposure among chocolate shoppers. However, the idea that cocoa comes in many varieties has been appearing in consumer contexts. One such is Mark Christian's Chocolate Atlas, which describes different strains.[8] Chocolate Atlas classifications are based on genetic research and regularly updated to reflect new findings. Perhaps because the site also reviews chocolate bars, its classification system makes explicit links between cocoa strains and the flavors they produce in chocolate. Christian divides cocoa into two major groupings: *primary strains*, defined by botanical and chemical characteristics of the cocoa, and *cultivar strains*, which, as the name implies, have been cultivated: intentionally nurtured by humans. Beyond the genetic clusters that Motamayor and his colleagues identified, this system allows for other factors that differentiate cocoa. One is that, just as with wine grapes, the terroir of a place contributes to the flavor of the cocoa that grows there. Used most often in French designations of agricultural goods, terroir means "taste of place." It reflects the fact that each aspect of a local ecosystem (including weather cycles, microbes and minerals present in the air, earth, and water, the structure of water systems, and so forth) interacts in a complex way with all the rest to produce a specific flavor in food that comes from that place. When genetically identical crops are grown in different places, terroir predicts they will taste different. Terroir also includes another aspect, which is people. Not only do the earth, rain, and sun mingle specifically in a particular place, but farmers manage that process to bring out desirable flavors in the foods they produce there. Human intention is just as important an element of terroir as the physical characteristics of place.

By dividing cocoa into primary and cultivar strains, the Chocolate Atlas offers a cocoa classification system that is similar to that for wine grapes, with their many varieties and flavor characteristics. Each cocoa strain can make for a very different chocolate experience, just like Cabernet Sauvignon and Chardonnay grapes make very different wines. Christian defines nine primary strains: Amazon, Amelonado, Beniano, Bicolor (actually a separate species, *Theobroma bicolor*), Contamana, Criollo, Grandiflorum (also a separate species), Guiana, and Nacional. Each has a distinct flavor profile when manufactured into chocolate, ranging from the well-known floral aspect of Nacional to the citrus "twang" and buttery nut of Grandiflorum, which, despite its impressive name, Christian calls "excruciatingly meek in bar form."[9]

As of 2016, Christian had identified thirty-seven cultivar strains, whose differences reflect some human intentionality, much as people have bred a single animal species, *Canis lupus familiaris*, into many dog breeds. Again, the flavor range is wide. The much-discussed CCN-51 hybrid from Ecuador (see chapter 8), bred for productivity and disease resistance, is "weak basal cocoa . . . lead & wood shavings . . . quite bitter."[10] In contrast, the celebrated Porcelana cultivar from Venezuela, among the most expensive cocoa in the world, makes chocolate with a "pure-flavored . . . buttery macadamia; berries 'n cream" flavor profile.[11] As both Motamayor's and Christian's classification systems suggest, cocoa is tremendously diverse, far beyond what a typical store shelf of chocolate bars reveals. And researchers continue to make new discoveries. For example, the notion that each *Theobroma cacao* tree is a certain type – say, Criollo or Amelonado – has been challenged, as trees have been discovered bearing pods of different types, and even single pods of multiple bean types. The species continues to reveal extraordinary plasticity in response to environmental changes and human intervention, and most of us have not experienced a fraction of that diversity in the form of chocolate. However, that is changing.

Single origin chocolate

As the science of classification evolves, some manufacturers are making it a priority to demonstrate cocoa's natural diversity in chocolate. These include craft makers, whose numbers have grown since the turn of the twenty-first century, especially in the US, but also in the UK and Western Europe. In 2015, industry analyst Curtis Vreeland estimated that US craft makers were selling chocolate to the value of $75 million to $100 million annually.[12] Most of these companies have at some point offered single origin chocolate, which is made using beans from one location. This can be as large as a country or as small as a plantation (in which case it is sometimes called "estate chocolate"). Often, the origin is a geographical feature, such as a valley or river. The purpose is to demonstrate the flavor of cocoa from that place. Two aspects of single origin chocolate are important to note. One is that bringing out flavors specific to place contrasts with the goal of multinational chocolate companies, which is to offer the same brand flavor, time and time again. The other is that single origin chocolate does not necessarily reflect cocoa classifications based on *type*, which involve some characteristic of the beans, from genes to typical flavor. Single origin chocolate is concerned with *place*. Because any one place (or even tree) can have different varieties of cocoa, single origin does not necessarily (or even often) describe chocolate made from a particular strain. Chocolate made with cocoa from Ecuador, for example, may include floral Nacional beans, but also the hybrid CCN-51.

The first contemporary single origin chocolate that gained widespread attention used cocoa from the Chuao Valley in Venezuela. Though others had made Chuao bars before, Amedei Chocolate in Italy helped popularize the origin, in part by acquiring, for a time, exclusive rights to purchase cocoa from this remote valley. Chuao beans are among the most prized of all cocoas. The valley itself is difficult to access, and recent political turmoil in Venezuela has made exporting Chuao beans even more challenging. Makers prize this cocoa not only because it is limited, but because the local river system deposits minerals in the earth that give most harvests a unique flavor of red and blue fruits.[13] This makes Chuao beans an excellent example of terroir in chocolate.

Another is Madagascar. In contrast to the rest of the cocoa world, where stocks of Criollo diminished during colonial periods, Madagascar growers maintained and at times even increased Criollo cultivation.[14] The natural ocean borders of Madagascar, an island-state off Africa's southeast coast, spared growers many of the disease and pest threats that decimated crops elsewhere. Madagascar cocoa is instantly recognizable for its bright, high citrus notes, which often include a tart cherry aspect or lime and cream. Papua New Guinea, where cocoa production diminished by conflict is now revitalizing, has also become a craft favorite. Papua New Guinea beans tend to be complex, making for chocolate whose flavor changes from start to finish. Nacional beans from Ecuador, with their distinctive floral notes, are also regaining the renown they once enjoyed. With such variety on offer in mature chocolate markets, shoppers are beginning once again to know their cocoa origin preferences. This is a shift away from the twentieth-century tendency (which still persists) to describe chocolate on the basis of its place of *manufacture*: Belgian (which, to me at least, signifies little regarding specific flavor or texture and usually has more to do with bonbons), Swiss (which tends to have a milky flavor and silky texture), or French (which typically has a smooth texture and dark roast). While country of manufacture can describe a distinct chocolate experience, cocoa's origin is just as important.

Beyond that, single origin chocolate can serve an educational function, especially as the places that retail and promote this type of chocolate, including festivals and local specialty shops, tend to offer consumers information about origins.[15] Perhaps most importantly, by indicating where the cocoa *grew*, single origin bars help to remind us that *chocolate starts on a tree*. From there, any consumer who is interested to learn more can expand from the experience that Ghana beans, for example, taste very different to those from Belize or Colombia, to understanding environmental differences among those places. By naming countries and regions, single origin bars also invite shoppers to consider the politics and economics of exporting cocoa. Venezuela is a useful example: when a favorite Chuao or Porcelana bar disappears from store shelves, consumers may learn that violent conflict has made accessing some of Venezuela's finest beans increasingly problematic. By offering a range of chocolate experiences that can change even day by day, single origin chocolate reminds us that there are real people, institutions, and power structures behind every bar.

Politics of fermentation and drying

Beyond cocoa classification schemes, two seemingly apolitical processing steps – fermentation and drying – also figure into quality politics. To understand how, we must first walk through the physical transformations that happen during both steps. During fermentation, the seeds with their sticky pulp are piled together, covered, and kept that way for about a week, sometimes less depending on variety and how fast the farmer needs to get her or his beans to market. Smallholders typically ferment cocoa in heaps on the ground, covering the beans with waxy plantain fronds, which hold in heat; this heap method is common in West Africa. Smallholders also ferment in baskets or plastic buckets, a method more common in Southeast Asia and the Americas, as well as Nigeria and Sierra Leone. Sometimes farmers stir the beans about halfway through to aerate them. Large fermentaries typically use the box method. Wet beans are piled into wooden boxes and covered to retain heat; the cocoa is often transferred through a series of boxes every day or two to aerate the beans.

In all cases, the goal is to encourage development of microorganisms, especially yeasts, which ferment sugars in the pulp.[16] Both acidity and temperature rise during this process, killing the seed, which means it can no longer germinate into a baby tree. As fermentation proceeds, chemical changes start to make the cocoa taste something like chocolate and turn it a chocolatey color. When a grader inspects the beans, the level of fermentation is visible: when cut in half, a well-fermented bean will typically be a uniform brown. Because most beans are violet in their raw state (a few are white or light rose), purple colors usually indicate the cocoa was not well fermented. Of course, as an organic process, fermentation does produce color variability, so the amount of purple is not an absolute flavor predictor, but it remains a key quality indicator for grading purposes. If beans are not fermented long enough (or, less often, if they are fermented for too long), that is also noticeable – and not deliciously so – in the chocolate's flavor.

The goal of drying is to reduce bean moisture levels to less than 10 percent, and ideally to around 6 or 7 percent. Where the main harvest takes place during a dry season, as it often does in West Africa, farmers can sundry their cocoa. They spread the beans out on tables or patios and turn or rake them so they dry evenly. Where harvest occurs during a wetter season, such as parts of South America, Southeast Asia, and elsewhere in Africa, beans may be dried mechanically, or on portable trays that can be moved or covered when rain comes. When artificial drying involves smoke, it runs the risk that the smoke will come into contact with the cocoa, giving the chocolate a barbecue-like flavor. Beans dried in this way may receive an inferior grade and lower price. As discussed in chapter 5, drying conditions are beyond any farmer's control. If the possibility for sun-drying does not exist, this can prevent farmers from selling cocoa that meets high quality expectations.

Researchers are currently paying a great deal of attention to fermentation, with the (perhaps unlikely) goal of standardizing and optimizing this complex biochemical process. My Google alert for "cocoa" regularly turns out biochemical studies of fermentation, dense with scientific terms, whereas I rarely come across works that address the *social* dynamics of these processing steps. This tells us that the research is skewed toward the hard sciences, with a goal of making a complex organic process more legible and purportedly controllable for people with the right disciplinary training, and perhaps limited socioeconomic relevance. For example, a recent article in a peer-reviewed journal on food science began with a clear and interesting history of cocoa fermentation in different contexts. Then it concluded that, "[t]o better control fermentation and the overall quality of the product . . . starter cultures like those used in other fermented food products" could replace cocoa's "traditional" spontaneous fermentation.[17] This suggestion valorizes an industrial model of food production that bears little resemblance to cocoa's smallholder structure. While earlier sections of the article had acknowledged the variability of cocoa farming across place and time, the conclusion involved top-down application of a standardized technique for improving quality – a recommendation that is unlikely to be practicable across three continents and five million growers.

Stephanie Barrientos's illuminating work offers an important and contrasting contribution to studies of fermentation. In research in Ghana and India, Barrientos found that while women participate in just about every farming step, they tend to do more work caring for young trees and in on-farm postharvest processing (that is, fermentation and drying). These stages are crucial to cocoa's potential to make high quality chocolate. While we cannot generalize to other contexts, Barrientos's evidence from Ghana showed that men are more likely to hasten drying so they can sell cocoa quickly, whereas women are more likely to invest the necessary time and energy in complete drying. Crucially, Barrientos reported that women farmers take this care because they "better understand the implications for quality."[18]

One of the longstanding realities of development work is that while academic studies, policy reports, and project plans pay a great deal of attention to women, it can be difficult to actually reach women through outsider initiatives. While women are responsible for many aspects of farming, and evidence suggests that they invest more in quality control than men do, the cocoa industry is highly masculinized. Men predominate at every level and, even when women are the intended beneficiaries of assistance, men often end up at the forefront. My own fieldwork in Ghana revealed that apart from explicit, well-directed efforts to empower women, most assistance went directly or indirectly to men. Barrientos found the same in her research on quality programs in Ghana. There is thus a mismatch between what the evidence shows – that women are more inclined to enhance quality – and where resources end up.

John Kehoe, Director of Sustainability at Guittard Chocolate in San Francisco, emphasizes that for Guittard, the social context of farming is foundational to producing a quality crop. On the basis of his experience sourcing cocoa from West Africa and elsewhere, Kehoe told me, "You can't have quality . . . if there are no schools, if there is no access to medicine, if women don't have more of a voice in their villages and family decisions. Quality is not just flavor, it's not just productivity. The social dynamic is very important."[19] Consideration of these social dynamics – particularly social relations of gender – must be a central feature of quality initiatives. If such endeavors are serious about cocoa's quality, they will prepare in advance to encounter and surmount sociocultural norms that may make it more difficult for women farmers to benefit from technical assistance.

Finally, how cocoa is fermented and dried – and by whom – impacts its trading potential. As discussed, craft makers often produce single origin chocolate that demonstrates distinct cocoa flavors. Though it may be otherwise in markets with which I am less familiar (for example, Colombia or Japan), among US makers, the preference – to the point of near exclusivity – is for centrally fermented cocoa. This is because when farmers undertake fermentation and drying, even with expertise, equipment, and ideal weather, they necessarily produce variable cocoa, at minimum because the microbes that ferment the beans differ from place to place. In contrast, a central fermentary can tailor fermentation technique and duration to local bean type, environmental conditions, and so forth, and then keep these constant across batches. This makes for a more internally consistent lot than on-farm fermentation can produce. I raise this point not to suggest that craft makers are deliberately excluding farmers who undertake fermentation and drying, but to show that those farmers *are* more limited in their opportunities to sell into the craft supply chain. At present, central fermentation happens mainly in Central and South America and the Caribbean. West African farmers, for the most part, ferment and dry their own cocoa, which makes it difficult for them to access the craft market.

TCHO Flavor Labs

In some parts of the chocolate industry, there is a growing awareness that cocoa quality is best served by empowering growers to take an active role in its governance. To achieve this, projects and programs must often begin by helping farmers fill a knowledge gap regarding how their crop translates into chocolate flavor. Among several projects focused on this outcome are TCHO Flavor Labs (see chapter 8 for others).[20] The San Francisco Bay Area-based chocolate company has built up educational programs in several origin countries that offer growers access to quality assessment technologies. Through its TCHOSource program, TCHO works with farmers on fermentation and drying, not only to refine those processes, but also to capture data that allow them to track the results of their methods.

One of the most compelling features of TCHOSource is its Flavor Labs, which it runs in partnership with Equal Exchange. TCHO has put together, in effect, tiny portable chocolate factories – small enough to fit on a tabletop – and installed them at origin sites. Where they lack firsthand knowledge of chocolate, it can be difficult for growers to translate daily farm management practices into addressing the flavor concerns of manufacturers. TCHO's Flavor Labs aim to bridge the gap, helping farmers make a meaningful connection between agricultural practices and a crop's chocolate flavor potential. When TCHO began its Flavor Labs, none of the participating producer groups was earning a premium for quality (though they may have been earning another premium, for Fairtrade, organic, or another certification). In just four years, by 2014, the six participating farmer groups in total had earned nearly $928,000 in quality premiums.[21] While TCHO has not yet published disaggregated information for participating groups or farm gate price, this total amount gives some indication of the economic value attached to quality – and the lost earning potential for farmers who do not have the opportunity to improve the quality of their crop.

CHAPTER EIGHT

Sustainable Futures

In this concluding chapter, I return to a pressing point that I made in the introduction: that because of climate change, land fatigue, tree vulnerability, and a host of other reasons, cocoa's long-term sustainability is threatened. While there is no doubt of this threat, here I emphasize that, as with every other issue I have addressed, discussions of cocoa sustainability are politically charged. Any individual, company, or organization will frame sustainability in a particular way, based on their position in the industry, and their reference points regarding the most important elements of the supply chain. As with quality, there is no single industry definition of cocoa sustainability.

I offer this one: sustainable cocoa is compensated well enough that farmers *want to* continue growing it as their primary employment, within a climatic environment that can support its commercial existence over the long term. Compensation calculations must include the price paid for cocoa, but also how much it costs to grow – including costs of farming inputs; political, social, and economic costs associated with land ownership and crop sale; personal energy costs of farming; and opportunity costs of growing something else, such as food for subsistence. I offer this definition not to suggest that everyone should adopt it, but as a starting point for assessing what *others* might mean when they talk about sustainability. In the remainder of this chapter, I describe some of the ways that cocoa sustainability is being addressed. If those ideas and actions do not seem to agree with my definition, then it is worth asking what other priorities or end goals are involved.

A world without chocolate

Driven by sales pressure to use sensationalist headlines, journalists often report only worst-case scenarios for cocoa, and nearly always frame these as threats to chocolate. After some of the largest companies, including Mars and Barry Callebaut, predicted that by 2020 there would be a 1 million MT cocoa shortfall compared to demand, reporters picked up on the story and invited readers to panic with the oft-repeated phrase, "The world is running out of chocolate."[1]

In such accounts, information about cocoa sustainability tends to come to public light framed by the priorities of the largest industry players. First, there is the issue of whether a 1 million MT deficit – an amount equal to nearly a quarter of 2016 total yields – is likely. In its less dramatic account, the ICCO also predicted a gap between supply and demand through 2023. By then, the organization estimated that total supply would be 4.68 million MT and total grindings, 4.78 million MT: a shortage of just 100,000 MT, which is a full order of magnitude smaller than the industry-predicted figure.[2] Second, there is the issue of framing. Arguably, the "problem" is not that the world is "running out of chocolate." The story of a supply shortfall might be more accurately framed as, "Farmers can't keep growing the amount of cocoa it takes for large companies to sustain increasing profits." When demand exceeds supply, cocoa's price goes up – and multinational companies stand to lose profitability. Gary Guittard, President and CEO of Guittard Chocolate, points out that higher cocoa prices attract more farmers to the crop, which means that when price remains high, supply *might* grow faster than expected. But any predicted shortfall sends the biggest players into a panic. In early 2016, when cocoa's price was still around $3,000 per MT, Guittard told me, "Right now the market's being driven on some levels by the big guys, fearful of the cocoa supply. Not so much that 'We won't have enough cocoa,' but that cocoa prices will go up. I think they want to head this off at the pass and say, 'Let's go and produce more cocoa so that we don't have this shortfall.'"[3]

As part of this endeavor, all the largest chocolate companies and cocoa processors have made sustainability commitments. Via Cocoa Life, Cadbury – under its parent company, Mondelēz – announced a $400 million investment in sustainability.[4] Both Hershey and Mars pledged to buy all of their cocoa from certified sustainable sources by 2020.[5] Nestlé set a 2016 objective to source almost a third of its cocoa under the terms of an internal plan to address supply chain challenges.[6] Among the processors, Olam and Cargill both detail expansive sustainability initiatives.[7] The largest, Barry Callebaut, has put forth an ambitious plan to make "sustainable chocolate the norm," including poverty alleviation for half a million growers and becoming "carbon and forest positive" by 2025.[8] It is critical to remember that, because sustainability is an important consumer buzzword, these companies no doubt deploy it as part of skillful marketing. On the other hand, they would not be investing at such levels if there were no real threat to cocoa.

Nevertheless, these companies have sophisticated strategies for protecting their margins in response to virtually any supply scenario. In the short-to-medium term, these include raising retail prices, decreasing product size, and lowering the cocoa content of products. Since Mondelēz's takeover of Cadbury, for example, the size of its Dairy Milk bar has shrunk, though its price remained constant.[9] Over the longer term, chocolate companies have encouraged consumers to think and behave differently around their "need" for chocolate. A cocoa shortfall is not about need in the same way as, for example, unmet demand for clean water. Chocolate is a luxury good and, however much we might crave it, we do not need it to survive. While people may desire more chocolate now than they did previously, this is not because humans spontaneously experienced new yearnings. As has virtually every consumer industry, chocolate has undergone a post-Fordist shift. Under Fordist conditions, consumer items come with few variable features, and the purchase of one item can typically satisfy a need. For example, to satisfy the desire to drive to work, a consumer can purchase one car. But if everyone buys just one item, and that item lasts for a long time, demand levels out and it becomes difficult for companies to increase profits. Under post-Fordist conditions, companies put in place strategies to retain profitability. On the production side, these usually involve cutting costs. On the consumption side, they include building in intentional and perceived obsolescence for products, so that we are compelled to buy them more frequently. Strategies also involve introducing more features or varieties to a product that used to have just one version. This can make it seem as if buying just one of any thing will not satisfy our needs. Faced with multiple versions, our desire for a product may become more tuned to its diverse offerings.

Chocolate was in some respects slower in its post-Fordist shift than other foods, such as breakfast cereals or orange juice. But it has caught up. For the largest companies to maintain profits, people can no longer consume chocolate as an occasional treat, and many more must buy it. So, chocolate now comes in many varieties, each serving a particular "desire," even as offering such chocolate may inspire that desire. Chocolates in different sizes, packaged to be consumed at specific moments (say, on the way to work or after exercise); chocolates in novel colors and shapes; chocolates that appear only during holidays; chocolates of varying percentages and origins; chocolates with an expanded range of inclusions (Mars's M&Ms are a great example): all of these are designed to make consumers buy more chocolate than they likely would have if there were fewer varieties on offer. Along with new markets in Asia and rising demand for dark chocolate (which requires a higher proportion of cocoa than milk chocolate), this post-Fordist shift has helped maintain and even grow demand for chocolate in mature markets.

Futures for cocoa

For many farmers, the priority is to maximize cocoa earnings. They can achieve this by securing a higher price for their cocoa, or by farming more land – but frequently neither of those options is within a grower's control. A third possibility is to increase yields from existing farmland. Thus, if a tree promises higher yields, regardless of other aspects, farmers may be willing to adopt it. Sometimes they have no choice, as when agricultural extension officers or sustainability initiatives distribute high-yield seedlings for free.

One of the most often discussed of these varieties is cocoa type CCN-51 (see figure 8.1). An agronomist from Ecuador, Homero Castro, developed CCN-51 (an acronym for Coleccion Castro Naranjal, and the number of tries it took him to create the hybrid) in the 1960s. Seeing the devastation wrought on Ecuador's crop from witches' broom, Castro became intent on developing a

Figure 8.1 CCN-51 cocoa variety, Ecuador © Bill Fredericks

hybrid that could resist the disease and produce more cocoa. After crossbreeding for more than a decade, he succeeded: CCN-51 produces anywhere from four to ten times the yields of other trees and is resistant to witches' broom. With such benefits, some farmers have elected to grow it; others receive CCN-51 seedlings without a full explanation of their properties. Regardless, CCN-51 has become a substantial portion of Ecuador's cocoa volumes. In 2011, estimates were that CCN-51 comprised a fifth of Ecuador's crop; by 2015, the estimated proportion had risen to 36 percent.[10] The strain has appeared in Central America, as well as Peru, Brazil, and possibly Indonesia. If indeed CCN-51 already comprises more than a third of Ecuador's crop, it could soon dominate not only that nation's cocoa, but further afield.

While CCN-51 offers yield benefits, it is also contentious, especially for those who prioritize cocoa's flavor potential. Castro's success in selecting for high yields and disease resistance meant sacrificing flavor. Mark Christian describes chocolate made with CCN-51 as weak and bitter, tasting of lead shavings. While Ecuador is a leading exporter of flavor beans, not all its crop receives this designation: the ICCO downgraded 25 percent of Ecuador's exports to bulk due to the prevalence of CCN-51. While specific fermentation techniques can reduce the acidic quality of chocolate made from CCN-51, several manufacturers have stated they will not use the beans, including Guittard and Lindt & Sprüngli. Mars, Mondelēz, Cargill, Barry Callebaut, and Blommer are all reported to use the beans, although in unknown quantities.[11] Choosing to use CCN-51 beans may signal that a company sees the strain as an option for maintaining cocoa as a viable commercial crop.

Another route to sustainability involves cultivating flavor strains. This path differs from efforts that focus on yields not only in the flavor aspect, but also in scale. Convincing farmers to grow trees that may produce lower yields, take more effort to care for, and are more susceptible to disease can be a harder sell. Because flavor strains generally fit that description, they will almost certainly remain at a much smaller scale than high-yield varieties. However, the benefits can be meaningful. Over the long term, cultivation of high-yield types has negative environmental impacts, including land fatigue and consequent reliance on expensive inputs. In contrast, one goal of flavor bean cultivation is to maintain diversity across *Theobroma cacao*, to generate varied chocolate experiences. Preserving diversity sometimes (though not always) involves using holistic farm management and organic growing methods that are, in the long term, healthier for trees, people, and environment.

Three organizations stand out for their commitment

to cocoa sustainability through flavor. One is the Cocoa of Excellence Programme, founded in 1998 and coordinated by Bioversity International.[12] The program solicits bean samples from grower organizations and processes promising ones into chocolate. Every two years, a panel of experts evaluates these and selects winners in Africa, Asia Pacific, Central America and the Caribbean, and South America, which are announced at the Salon du Chocolat in Paris. The program has wide support, from the ICCO and Cocoa Research Centre at the University of the West Indies, to chocolate companies Guittard, Mars, Nestlé, Barry Callebaut, and Valrhona, equipment manufacturer CocoaTown, and Lutheran World Relief. This suggests that many industry players, with priorities from poverty alleviation to equipment sales, see flavor bean cultivation as a pathway to sustainability.

Another is the Heirloom Cacao Preservation Fund (HCP), a collaboration between the Fine Chocolate Industry Association (FCIA) and the USDA that began in 2012.[13] HCP also solicits samples of high quality cocoa, which it processes into chocolate for tasting by an expert panel. The USDA analyzes and records sample genetics, creating a database of cocoa genotypes. While the word "heirloom" suggests that the beans have some historical quality, designation is based on flavor. Once a strain receives heirloom designation, HCP works to protect and propagate it, and to link its growers to premium market channels. The third organization, the Fine Cacao and Chocolate Institute (FCCI), works in a different way.[14] Unlike coffee, for which the Q Grader program provides an internationally recognized method for assessing quality, there is no common language or agreed-upon standard for describing cocoa flavor. The industry makes a gross distinction between bulk and flavor beans, and differentiates among bulk grades in futures trading. But when it comes to qualitative aspects – do beans taste nutty or fruity or pleasantly like tobacco? – there are no universal criteria. FCCI is working to clarify and codify this.

Taste is subjective. You and I might taste different flavors in a chocolate depending on our palates, what we ate previously, the time of day, our hunger levels, and so forth. Moreover, chocolate's many aspects, from the first bouquet of scent to how fast it melts in our mouths, combine to produce a holistic taste experience. But there are methods for teasing out and identifying flavor components objectively. To become proficient in these, one must undergo organoleptic calibration exercises, learning to identify patterns of flavor within a cocoa sample. FCCI is adapting coffee assessment methods to cocoa as well as overcoming cocoa-specific challenges: for example, processing beans to a liquor or semi-liquor state at an appropriate scale for training tasters, and determining vocabulary to consistently describe taste experiences. The goal is to create a common language that both buyers and sellers can use. FCCI conducts trainings for people who buy cocoa and make chocolate, so they can be more discriminating purchasers of beans. But it also trains growers, who can then be more knowledgeable sellers. Because cocoa farmers often have little experience with industrial bar chocolate, they usually lack a way to translate the flavor qualities of their beans into terms that are meaningful for the final product. By processing micro-batches of beans into liquor to taste, and developing a database of flavor notes with a common language to describe them, FCCI imagines a future where farmers can talk as knowledgeably about their crop's potential as those at the other end of the value chain. With this knowledge, farmers will be in a stronger position to manage defects, improve flavor quality, and negotiate price.

Both high-yield and flavor approaches need to succeed to fulfill my definition of sustainability. While I have described them as distinct or even contrasting, some experts believe it is possible to achieve healthy, high-yielding crops and flavor on the same farm. Several strains recently developed in Costa Rica, called (unfortunately for marketing purposes) R-1, R-4, and R-6 at the Centro Agronómico Tropical de Investigación y Enseñanza (CATIE), offer high yields, resistance to frosty pod rot, and superior flavor. Indeed, R-4 and R-6 have won awards at the Salon du Chocolat in Paris.[15] Both approaches also need to succeed in West Africa. The region produces mainly hardy Amelonado types, which do not usually rank among flavor beans, and flavor initiatives are geographically much more focused on Central and South America, and the Caribbean. As of 2016, for example, the HCP had never awarded heirloom status to an African cocoa. Yet while most cocoa from the region does not offer particularly novel flavors, West African cocoa has been the century-long foundation of the industry because *it tastes good*. The region deserves attention to – and investment in – maintaining its beloved flavor as a sustainability option.

Vertically integrated companies offer another holistic version of cocoa sustainability. Such companies bring the two ends of the commodity chain – cocoa and chocolate – together into one business. In the most condensed version, the same person (or a small group) is both farmer and chocolate maker. These companies are presently most common in the US state of Hawaii. There, Bob Cooper of the Original Hawaiian Chocolate Factory was among the earliest to farm cocoa and make chocolate locally.[16] More recently, Seneca Klassen of Lonohana Hawaiian Estate Chocolate,[17] and Dave Elliott and Nat Bletter of Madre Chocolate,[18] have done the same. Other companies integrate sourcing and manufacturing to a lesser extent, but still keep the supply chain local. The Grenada Chocolate Company has a local buying cooperative for organic cocoa, from which it produces chocolate on the island for sale locally and abroad. In a remarkable move to reduce the company's carbon footprint from shipping, the company's late co-founder, Mott Green, arranged to have bars transported to the US and Europe on sailing vessels. In Vietnam, Marou Chocolate works closely with local growers to source cocoa and make chocolate.[19] Kallari Chocolate buys cocoa and manufactures chocolate in Ecuador.[20] In Accra, '57 Chocolate uses high quality beans sourced domestically in Ghana.

In all these companies, manufacture happens in close proximity to farming, making it that much less likely that any participant can remain far removed from what is happening at other points in the supply chain. This can help make everyone involved in the process – cocoa growers, buyers, factory workers, management, distributors, retailers – aware of the challenges that others face. When the supply chain is more far-flung, as it typically is for cocoa and chocolate, then at every step from farm to retail, everyday reality becomes more alien from the stage before. For example, it would likely be challenging for the managing director of a cocoa processor in the Netherlands to viscerally comprehend the everyday life of a cocoa farmer in Ivory Coast, and vice versa. But, of course, that manager works for a company that has more influence in the industry than the cocoa farmer. Arguably, if the goal is to sustain cocoa, then that manager has a responsibility to do her or his best to comprehend the farmer's reality, the better to enact solutions that will be viable at the foundation of the supply chain.

This brings me to my final point. Perhaps the most important element of cocoa's sustainability is that farmers regard their work as honorable and valued. Children of farmers prefer to work in urban areas and see little fulfillment in following in their parents' footsteps. Parents do not necessarily disagree, especially if their own crop is faltering, or if they do not perceive anyone else in the industry, from buyers onward, as valuing their labor. My experience with growers in West Africa is that they see farming as a low-skill endeavor, and everything that happens to cocoa beyond their farms as technologically exciting, performed by respected experts. After working for more than a decade with Kuapa Kokoo in Ghana, Sophi Tranchell, Managing Director of Divine Chocolate, told me, "We need to get the industry to a place where if a farmer's child comes home and says *they* want to be a cocoa farmer, the parents wouldn't be worried and would actually be pleased."[21]

For that to happen, then every actor in this industry must convey that every step of the process, from planting a tree to selling a bar of chocolate, is inherently valuable. Though incomes for farmers and chocolate makers or company owners are unlikely to equalize, we can still emphasize that *all types of labor* deserve attention and appropriate compensation. There is no reason that developing a brand slogan or bar recipe should earn anyone more respect than a lifetime of pruning and weeding *Theobroma cacao*. From there, the conversation begins. For cocoa farmers to make a dignified living and for consumers to continue enjoying chocolate, sustainability must involve placing the highest possible value on cocoa at every step, from seed to taste bud.

Notes

I INTRODUCTION

1 One of the most detailed studies is William Gervase Clarence-Smith, *Cocoa and Chocolate, 1765–1914* (London: Routledge, 2000).

2 Eline Poelmans and Johan Swinnen, "A Brief Economic History of Chocolate," in *The Economics of Chocolate*, eds. Mara P. Squicciarini and Johan Swinnen (Oxford: Oxford University Press, 2016), 24.

3 I discuss this further in "Invisible West Africa: The Politics of Single Origin Chocolate," *Gastronomica: The Journal of Critical Food Studies* 13, no. 3 (2013).

4 Catherine Araujo Bonjean and Jean-François Brun, "Concentration and Price Transmission in the Cocoa-Chocolate Chain," in *Economics of Chocolate*, 350.

5 Emmanuel K. Dogbevi, "Africa Produces 75% of Cocoa But Gets 2% of $100b Chocolate Market Revenue," *Ghana Business News*, May 25, 2016, https://www.ghanabusinessnews.com/2016/05/25/157624.

6 Poelmans and Swinnen provide consumption rates in "Brief Economic History," 35–8. Their 2010 estimates are slightly higher than those in Euromonitor 2014, as reported by Oliver Nieburg in "The Chocolate League Tables 2014: Top 20 Consuming Nations," *ConfectioneryNews*, October 9, 2014, http://www.confectionerynews.com/Markets/Chocolate-consumption-by-country-2014.

7 A classic volume is *Chocolate in Mesoamerica: A Cultural History of Cacao*, ed. Cameron L. McNeil (Gainesville: University Press of Florida, 2006). Carla D. Martin and Kathryn E. Sampeck provide a recent account, which includes cocoa's role as

flavoring, in "The Bitter and Sweet of Chocolate in Europe," paper presented at The Social Meaning of Food Workshop, Institute for Sociology, Hungarian Academy of Sciences, June 16–17, 2015, http://www.socio.hu/uploads/files/2015en_food/chocolate.pdf.

8 *Sacred Gifts, Profane Pleasures: A History of Tobacco and Chocolate in the Atlantic World* (Ithaca: Cornell University Press, 2008). In a somewhat contrasting account, Sophie D. Coe and Michael D. Coe emphasize how early European adopters transformed cocoa drinks to suit their own tastes; see *The True History of Chocolate*, second edition (London: Thames & Hudson, 2007), chs. 4 and 5.

9 Coe and Coe, *True History*, ch. 8. For detailed histories of early (and enduring) industrial chocolate companies, see Deborah Cadbury, *Chocolate Wars: From Cadbury to Kraft* (London: Harper Press, 2011), and Michael D'Antonio, *Hershey: Milton S. Hershey's Extraordinary Life of Wealth, Empire, and Utopian Dreams* (London: Simon & Schuster, 2006).

10 I put quotation marks around "raw" to signal that we cannot consume chocolate raw in the same way as, for example, a carrot, which can be eaten immediately once dug from the ground. Cocoa seeds can be consumed from the pod, but they move through a great deal of processing to become bar chocolate (see chapter 3), thus troubling the notion that chocolate can be considered "raw." Moreover, the usual starting point for transforming cocoa into chocolate is fermentation, which is typically carried out at temperatures higher than 40° Celsius (104° Fahrenheit) – the point at which foods are commonly considered to go from raw to cooked.

11 Oliver Nieburg, "Power of the Dark Side: Technavio Reveals Forecasts and Growth Drivers for Global Dark Chocolate Market," *ConfectioneryNews*, July 29, 2015, http://www.confectionerynews.com/Markets/Dark-chocolate-market-sales-forecasts-Technavio-predictions.

12 On China, see Lawrence L. Allen, *Chocolate Fortunes: The Battle for the Hearts, Minds, and Wallets of China's Consumers* (New York: AMACOM, 2010), and Fan Li and Di Mo, "The Burgeoning Chocolate Market in China," in *Economics of Chocolate*. On India, see Emma Janssen and Olivia Riera, "Too Hot to Handle: The Explosive Growth of Chocolate in India," in *Economics of Chocolate*.

13 See Poelmans and Swinnen, "Brief Economic History," 37, table 2.12.

14 Seneshaw Tamru and Johan Swinnen, "Back to the Roots: Growth in Cocoa and Chocolate Consumption in Africa," in *Economics of Chocolate*, 440, 444.

15 Olam is based in Singapore, which, at just over 1° N latitude, is within cocoa's growing range; however, the city-state is too small to dedicate land to it.

16 *QBCS*, XLIII, table 1.

17 ICCO, *The Cocoa Market Situation* (July 2014), 3, https://www.icco.org/about-us/international-cocoa-agreements/cat_view/30-related-documents/45-statistics-other-statistics.html.

18 John H. Bowers et al., "The Impact of Plant Diseases on World Chocolate Production," *Plant Health Progress*, June 14, 2001, http://www.apsnet.org/publications/apsnetfeatures/Pages/WorldChocolateProduction.aspx.

19 "New Hope for the Future of Chocolate," *Phys.org*, January 20, 2017, https://phys.org/news/2017-01-future-chocolate.html.

20 Martin Gilmour et al., "Minimizing the Risk of Spreading Cocoa Swollen Shoot Virus Disease," World Agroforestry Centre (2011), http://www.worldagroforestry.org/sites/default/files/Brochure-Cocoa-Swollen-Shoot-Virus-Disease.pdf.

21 See http://www.cabi.org/isc/datasheet/7017.

22 "Scientists Date the Origin of the Cacao Tree to 10 Million Years Ago," *Phys.org*, November 10, 2015, http://phys.org/news/2015-11-scientists-date-cacao-tree-million.html.

23 Jean-Marc Anga, *The World Cocoa Economy: Current Status, Challenges and Prospects* (April 2014), 21, http://unctad.org/meetings/en/Presentation/SUC_MEM2014_09042014_ICCO.pdf.

24 For a recent scholarly assessment, see James Sumberg, Thomas Yeboah, Justin Flynn, and Nana Akua Anyidoho, "Young People's Perspectives on Farming in Ghana: A Q Study," *Food Security* 9 (2017), http://link.springer.com/article/10.1007/s12571-016-0646-y. For a journalistic account, see Maggie Fick, "Ageing Cocoa Farmers Pose Risk for Ghana Industry," *Financial Times*, July 12, 2015, https://www.ft.com/content/d9cb0d1c-26e7-11e5-bd83-71cb60e8f08c.

25 Gabriel Ewepu, "FG Says Nigeria to Become World's Largest Cocoa Producer," *Vanguard*, January 13, 2017, http://www.

vanguardngr.com/2017/01/fg-says-nigeria-become-worlds-largest-cocoa-producer.

26 Björn Beckman, *Organising the Farmers: Cocoa Politics and National Development in Ghana* (Uppsala: Scandinavian Institute of African Studies, 1976).

27 For example, Tom Philpott, "Bloody Valentine: Child Slavery in Ivory Coast's Cocoa Fields," *Mother Jones*, February 14, 2012, http://www.motherjones.com/tom-philpott/2012/02/ivory-coast-cocoa-chocolate-child-slavery; Sam Webb, "Is Your Chocolate Bar Worth a Child's Life?" *Daily Mail Online*, February 27, 2014, http://www.dailymail.co.uk/news/article-2569091/Is-chocolate-bar-worth-childs-life-Documentary-lays-bare-child-slavery-West-Africas-cocoa-plantations-free-them.html; Fair Trade USA, "Is There Child Labor in Your Chocolate?" *Huffpost*, February 9, 2016, http://www.huffingtonpost.com/fair-trade-usa/is-there-child-labor-in-y_b_9169898.html.

28 See http://www.slavefreechocolate.org/about-us-1.

29 See http://www.slavefreechocolate.org/ethical-chocolate-companies.

30 For example, the International Cocoa Initiative (ICI), an organization dedicated to addressing child labor, works in those two countries; see http://www.cocoainitiative.org/about-ici/about-us.

31 See Clarence-Smith, *Cocoa and Chocolate*, ch. 8.

32 International Labour Office (ILO), *Marking Progress Against Child Labour: Global Estimates and Trends 2000–2012*, vii, 4–5, http://www.cocoainitiative.org/wp-content/uploads/2016/07/ILO_progress_221513.pdf.

33 For me, some of the most instructive works about how Western media has portrayed black African people as primitive include: Lucy Jarosz, "Constructing the Dark Continent: Metaphor as Geographic Representation of Africa," *Geografiska Annaler* 74 (1992); Curtis Keim, *Mistaking Africa: Curiosities and Inventions of the American Mind*, second edition (Boulder: Westview Press, 2009); Paul S. Landau and Deborah D. Kaspin, eds., *Images and Empires: Visuality in Colonial and Postcolonial Africa* (Berkeley: University of California Press, 2002); Catherine A. Lutz and Jane L. Collins, *Reading National Geographic* (Chicago: University of Chicago Press, 1993); Anne McClintock, *Imperial*

Leather: Race, Gender and Sexuality in the Colonial Conquest (New York: Routledge, 1995); and work by the Modern Girl Around the World research group: Tani Barlow, Madeleine Yue Dong, Uta Poiger, Priti Ramamurthy, Lynn M. Thomas, and Alys Eve Weinbaum, including the edited volume *The Modern Girl Around the World: Consumption, Modernity, and Globalization* (Durham: Duke University Press, 2008), and especially Lynn M. Thomas's work.

34 See Kevin Bales and Ron Soodalter, *The Slave Next Door: Human Trafficking and Slavery in America Today* (Berkeley: University of California Press, 2009), and Kevin Bales, *Disposable People: New Slavery in the Global Economy* (Berkeley: University of California Press, 1999).

35 See my article, "'Artisan' as Brand: Adding Value in a Craft Chocolate Community," *Food, Culture & Society: An International Journal of Multidisciplinary Research* 20, no. 1 (2017).

36 See Josée Johnston and Shyon Baumann, *Foodies: Democracy and Distinction in the Gourmet Foodscape* (New York: Routledge, 2010).

37 Sumberg et al., "Young People's Perspectives."

38 Mark Babatunde, "Meet 2 Sisters Turning Cocoa Beans into Chocolate Bars in Ghana," *Face2FaceAfrica*, February 8, 2017, https://face2faceafrica.com/article/57-chocolate-ghana.

39 I draw upon my fieldwork to analyze cocoa power and politics in this book, and for quotes (I have changed some names and other identifying details). In 2005, I conducted six months of doctoral research in Ghana, which included interviews with growers, buyers, and supply chain managers in the Western and Ashanti regions. I researched food culture, including a survey of household expenditure, interviews about food preferences, and participant observation. I surveyed retail outlets in villages, towns, and cities for chocolate availability and price. I visited cocoa processing facilities in Tema and Takoradi and interviewed factory managers. In 2013, I conducted a gender program impact assessment in Ghana for Divine Chocolate and Twin, a London-based development-through-trade charity. Our research team surveyed 258 farmers in the Western and Ashanti regions, including 218 women and 40 men. I also draw upon briefer periods of fieldwork, conferences, farm visits, and factory visits in Hawaii, Malaysia, UK (especially London), US

(especially Seattle, San Francisco, and New York), Nigeria, and Sierra Leone from 2005 to 2017. In the Acknowledgments, I note interviews conducted specifically for this book.

40 See Jean Marie Allman, "The Youngmen and the Porcupine: Class, Nationalism and Asante's Struggle for Self-Determination, 1954–57," *Journal of African History* 31 (1990); Jean Allman and Victoria Tashjian, *"I Will Not Eat Stone": A Woman's History of Colonial Asante* (Portsmouth, NH: Heinemann Press, 2000); and Gwendolyn Mikell, *Cocoa and Chaos in Ghana* (New York: Paragon House, 1989).

41 *Tomatoland: How Modern Industrial Agriculture Destroyed Our Most Alluring Fruit* (Kansas City: Andrews McMeel, 2011).

42 Johnny Lieu, "24-Karat Gold Kit Kat is for the Chocolate Lover Who Has it All," *Mashable*, January 21, 2016, http://mashable.com/2016/01/21/gold-kit-kat-chocolate/#QKObl12gqZq0.

43 "Diamond-Topped Chocolate Cake on Sale as Japan Gears up for Valentine's Day," *Japan Times*, January 26, 2016, http://www.japantimes.co.jp/news/2016/01/26/business/diamond-topped-chocolate-cake-sale-japan-gears-valentines-day/#.WJ8lXJJsut8.

44 Jerry Toth, "Vintage Dark Chocolate Aged for 18 Months Fetches $345 per Bar," *PRWeb*, January 27, 2016, http://www.prweb.com/releases/ToakChocolate/01/prweb13168913.htm.

45 Ian Smillie, *Diamonds* (Cambridge: Polity, 2014).

46 A good place to start is Coe and Coe, *True History*, 18. For a history of the word "chocolate," see the section "Crossing the Language Barrier," ch. 4.

2 WORLD COCOA MAP

1 Allen M. Young, *The Chocolate Tree: A Natural History of Cacao*, revised and expanded edition (Gainesville: University Press of Florida, 2007), xi.

2 For historical uses of cocoa bark, leaves, pulp, and seeds, see Nathaniel Bletter and Douglas C. Daly, "Cacao and Its Relatives in South America," in *Chocolate in Mesoamerica*. See also John S. Henderson et al., "Chemical and Archaeological Evidence for the Earliest Cacao Beverages," *PNAS* 104 (2007), http://www.pnas.org/content/104/48/18937.full.

3 Young details these possibilities in *Chocolate Tree*, chs. 1 and 2.
4 For example, Coe and Coe, *True History*.
5 Dorie Reents-Budet, "The Social Context of Kakaw Drinking among the Ancient Maya," in *Chocolate in Mesoamerica*.
6 Laura Caso Barrera and Mario Aliphat F., "The Itza Maya Control over Cacao: Politics, Commerce, and War in the Sixteenth and Seventeenth Centuries," in *Chocolate in Mesoamerica*, 296. See also Martin and Sampeck, "Bitter and Sweet," 39.
7 William R. Fowler, "Cacao Production, Tribute, and Wealth in Sixteenth-Century Izalcos, El Salvador," in *Chocolate in Mesoamerica*.
8 See Sophie D. Coe, *America's First Cuisines* (Austin: University of Texas Press, 1994), and Norton, *Sacred Gifts*.
9 Introduction to *Chocolate in Mesoamerica*, 14.
10 Norton, *Sacred Gifts*, 35.
11 For example, Maricel Presilla, *The New Taste of Chocolate*, revised edition (Berkeley: Ten Speed Press, 2009), 22; Norton, *Sacred Gifts*, 30–6; Coe and Coe, *True History*, 72–3.
12 Patricia L. Crown and W. Jeffrey Hurst, "Evidence of Cacao Use in the Prehispanic American Southwest," *PNAS* 106 (2009), http://www.pnas.org/content/106/7/2110.abstract.
13 See http://www.icco.org/faq/53-cocoa-beans/116-fine-or-flavour-cocoa.html.
14 Young, *Chocolate Tree*, 19.
15 Coe and Coe, *True History*, 108–9.
16 The source most frequently cited for these figures is *Historia general y natural de las Indias*, by Gonzalo Fernández de Oviedo y Valdes, chronicler for the Spanish Crown. See Young, *Chocolate Tree*, 29–30; Coe and Coe, *True History*, 59.
17 Coe and Coe, *True History*, 148–52.
18 *Sacred Gifts*, 231–7.
19 "The Surprising History of London's Lost Chocolate Houses," *Telegraph*, December 13, 2013, http://www.telegraph.co.uk/travel/destinations/europe/uk/london/10515620/The-surprising-history-of-Londons-lost-chocolate-houses.html.
20 Clarence-Smith and François Ruf, "Cocoa Pioneer Fronts: The Historical Determinants," in *Cocoa Pioneer Fronts since 1800: The Role of Smallholders, Planters and Merchants*, ed. William Gervase Clarence-Smith (London: Macmillan, 1996), 3.

21 Clarence-Smith details the histories of African slave labor, Amerindian labor, and indentured workers from Asia for many more cocoa regions than I have summarized here in *Cocoa and Chocolate*, ch. 8.

22 *Cocoa and Chocolate*, 200.

23 Emma Robertson, *Chocolate, Women and Empire: A Social and Cultural History* (Manchester: Manchester University Press, 2009), ch. 1.

24 Virginia Westbrook, "Role of Trade Cards in Marketing Chocolate During the Late 19th Century," in *Chocolate: History, Culture, and Heritage*, eds. Louis Evan Grivetti and Howard-Yana Shapiro (Hoboken, NJ: John Wiley & Sons, 2009).

25 *True History*, 244–6. See also Cadbury, *Chocolate Wars*, 12–13.

26 Poelmans and Swinnen, "Brief Economic History," 21–2.

27 Poelmans and Swinnen, "Brief Economic History," 24.

28 Lowell J. Satre, *Chocolate on Trial: Slavery, Politics & the Ethics of Business* (Athens: Ohio University Press, 2005), 19.

29 Satre, *Chocolate on Trial*, 146.

30 *Cocoa and Chocolate*, 221–3.

31 *The Gold Coast Cocoa Farmer: A Preliminary Survey* (London: Oxford University Press, 1956), and *The Migrant Cocoa-Farmers of Southern Ghana: A Study in Rural Capitalism* (Cambridge: Cambridge University Press, 1963).

32 See http://www.koko.gov.my/lkm/industry/statistic/p_cocoabean.cfm.

33 *QBCS*, XLIII, table 38.

34 *QBCS*, XLIII, tables 4 and 38.

35 *QBCS*, XLIII, table 4.

36 See the brand's official Tumblr page, http://snickers.tumblr.com, and Adbrands's analysis of the "When You're Hungry" campaign, http://www.adbrands.net/us/snickers_us.htm.

3 STAGES OF SWEET

1 For a visual illustration of chocolate processing, see Megan Giller, *Bean-to-Bar Chocolate: America's Craft Chocolate Revolution* (North Adams, MA: Storey, 2017), especially 24–5 and 37.

2 Personal communication, April 8, 2016.

3 See http://www.dandelionchocolate.com.

4 See https://www.chocolats-pralus.com/en/index.php.

5 See http://www.mrchocolate.com.

6 Personal communication, April 8, 2016.

7 Personal communication, March 31, 2016.

8 After this step, tempering, packaging (in vacuum versus air), and aging chocolate also contribute to flavor.

9 See http://frescochocolate.com/collections/flight-of-papua-new-guinea.

10 Bonjean and Brun, "Concentration and Price Transmission," 351–2.

11 Giulia Meloni and Johan Swinnen, "Chocolate Regulations," in Economics of Chocolate, 287–90.

12 For a full technical discussion of cocoa butter, see Stephen T. Beckett, The Science of Chocolate, second edition (Cambridge: Royal Society of Chemistry, 2008), ch. 6.

13 Meloni and Swinnen, "Chocolate Regulations," 290–1.

14 For the US, see Food and Drug Administration (FDA), "Guidance for Industry: Standard of Identity for White Chocolate," https://www.fda.gov/food/guidanceregulation/ guidancedocumentsregulatoryinformation/labelingnutrition/ ucm059076.htm. For the EU, see Food Standards Agency, "Quick Guide to Chocolate," http://tna.europarchive. org/20120419000433/http://www.food.gov.uk/multimedia/ pdfs/publication/chocolatefactsheet0210.pdf.

15 Cocoa and Chocolate; tariff and other trade details are from chs. 3 and 4.

16 Clarence-Smith, Cocoa and Chocolate, 48.

17 Cocoa and Chocolate, 53.

18 See http://agoa.info/about-agoa.html.

19 See http://agoa.info/about-agoa/product-eligibility.html.

20 USITC, AGOA (2014), 57, https://www.usitc.gov/ publications/332/pub4461.pdf.

21 QBCS, XLIII, table 2.

22 QBCS, XLIII, table 3.

23 See my article, "Racing the Melt: The Quest for Heat-Resistant Chocolate," Conversation, July 28, 2015, http://theconversation. com/racing-the-melt-the-quest-for-heat-resistant-chocolate-44119.

24 Edward George, Overview of Global Cocoa, Coffee and Sugar

Markets (November 2013), 6, http://www.globalgrainevents.com/pdfs/Geneva%202013/EdwardGeorgeEcobankOverview.pdf.

25 *QBCS*, XLIII, table 5.

26 Emmanuel Tumanjong, "Cameroon's Processed Cocoa Beans Up 49% from Year Earlier," *ADVFN*, August 9, 2015, http://uk.advfn.com/news/DJN/2015/article/68095250.

27 See https://www.barry-callebaut.com/news/2007/02/barry-callebaut-inaugurates-second-cocoa-bean-processing-line-tema-factory-ghana and https://www.barry-callebaut.com/news/2007/07/barry-callebaut-expands-its-operations-ivory-coast.

28 Bonjean and Brun, "Concentration and Price Transmission," 345.

29 See https://www.barry-callebaut.com/news/2007/02/barry-callebaut-inaugurates-second-cocoa-bean-processing-line-tema-factory-ghana.

30 *Chocolate Nations: Living and Dying for Cocoa in West Africa* (London: Zed Books, 2011), 89.

31 Barry Callebaut: https://www.barry-callebaut.com/news/2007/02/barry-callebaut-inaugurates-second-cocoa-bean-processing-line-tema-factory-ghana; Cargill: https://www.cargill.com/worldwide/ghana.

32 Bonjean and Brun, "Concentration and Price Transmission," 345.

33 Ryan, *Chocolate Nations*, 89.

34 See https://www.barry-callebaut.com/news/2007/07/barry-callebaut-expands-its-operations-ivory-coast.

35 See http://www.goldentreeghana.com.

36 See http://www.57chocolategh.com.

37 Personal communication, May 3, 2017.

38 See Cadbury, *Chocolate Wars*, and D'Antonio, *Hershey*.

4 POWER IN THE MARKET

1 *Chocolate Fortunes*.

2 See http://data.worldbank.org/country/cote-divoire.

3 R. J. Whitehead, "Indians Getting Sweet on Chocolate Thanks to Cadbury Revolution," *ConfectioneryNews*, September 23, 2014,

http://www.confectionerynews.com/Markets/Indians-getting-sweet-on-chocolate-thanks-to-Cadbury-revolution.

4 Oliver Nieburg, "Untapped Potential for Chocolate Makers in Rural India, Says ValueNotes," *ConfectioneryNews*, September 25, 2014, http://www.confectionerynews.com/Markets/Rural-India-chocolate-market-set-for-growth.

5 Joël Glenn Brenner, *The Emperors of Chocolate: Inside the Secret World of Hershey & Mars* (New York: Broadway Books, 2000).

6 Emiko Terazono, "Welcome to the World of Big Chocolate," *Financial Times*, December 18, 2014, https://www.ft.com/content/80e196cc-8538-11e4-ab4e-00144feabdc0.

7 "Barry Callebaut to Buy Petra Foods Cocoa Unit for $950 Million," *Reuters*, December 12, 2012, http://uk.reuters.com/article/uk-barrycallebaut-petrafoods-idUKBRE8BB0A320121212. Note: the final acquisition price was $860 million.

8 See the diagram in the section "What We Do," http://annual-report-2015–16.barry-callebaut.com.

9 For example, Elisa Depypere, "10 Facts about Barry Callebaut," *Belgian Smaak*, April 27, 2015, http://www.belgiansmaak.com/largest-chocolate-factory-in-the-world-barry-callebaut-chocolates.

10 See http://www.cargill.co.uk/en/index.jsp.

11 See https://www.cargill.com/news/releases/2015/NA31877259.jsp. Using published estimates that the three largest processors command 60 percent market share, of which Barry Callebaut accounts for 25 percent and Olam 16 percent, I calculated Cargill's share to be 19 percent.

12 Raymond Leung, "Analysts Updates: Olam International to be 3rd Largest Cocoa Processor," *Shares Investment*, December 24, 2014, http://www.sharesinv.com/articles/2014/12/24/olam-third-largest-cocoa-processor.

13 See http://olamgroup.com.

14 See https://makechocolatefair.org/issues/cocoa-prices-and-income-farmers-0.

15 See https://www.behindthebrands.org/en-us/scorecard.

16 Cocoa seasons differ across growing regions, but the main West Africa harvest, from September through March, is most important to supply cycles. Chocolate's season extends over roughly the same period in North America and Europe, from Halloween at the end of October, through Easter and Passover in March or April, and stretching into the May holidays. While

summer is a retail "dead season" for chocolate, there can be peaks in Europe during the holiday months.

17 Robin Dand, *The International Cocoa Trade*, third edition (Cambridge: Woodhead, 2011), 209.

18 Bonjean and Brun, "Concentration and Price Transmission," 342.

19 See https://www.grenadachocolate.com.

20 Matthew Mitchell, "Land Tenure Reform and Politics in Post-Conflict Côte d'Ivoire: A Precarious Peace in the Western Cocoa Regions," *Canadian Journal of African Studies* 48, no. 2 (2014), 208–9.

21 Richard Anderson, "Ivory Coast Crisis: Impact on the International Cocoa Trade," *BBC*, March 9, 2011, http://www.bbc.co.uk/news/business-12677418.

22 Órla Ryan, "Cocoa Wars: Ivory Coast 'Nationalises' Its Beans," *Financial Times*, March 8, 2011, https://next.ft.com/content/2380a568-49b4-11e0-acf0-00144feab49a.

23 Emiko Terazono, "Cocoa Succumbs to Commodity Rout," *Financial Times*, January 22, 2016, https://www.ft.com/content/db82f87e-c0fa-11e5-846f-79b0e3d20eaf.

24 Ange Aboa, "Worst Harmattan Winds in Decades to Slash Ivory Coast Cocoa Mid-Crop," *Reuters*, February 2, 2016, http://www.reuters.com/article/cocoa-ivorycoast-midcrop-idUSL8N15H37L.

25 Given the scale of imports and grindings in the EU, and the fact that three producers (Ivory Coast, Cameroon, and Togo) use a version of the CFA franc (West African or Central Africa), which is pegged to the euro, it is also possible to purchase cocoa contracts denominated in euros, though few traders do.

26 Anga, *World Cocoa Economy*, 19.

27 "The Dynamics of the World Cocoa Price," in *Economics of Chocolate*, 322–3.

28 Richard Tyler and Laura Roberts, "Cocoa King Anthony Ward is Hungry for African Food Production," *Telegraph*, July 19, 2010, http://www.telegraph.co.uk/finance/markets/7897389/Cocoa-king-Anthony-Ward-is-hungry-for-African-food-production.html. According to my calculations, these bars would need to be milk chocolate of much less than 50 percent cocoa solids.

29 Julia Werdigier and Julie Creswell, "Trader's Cocoa Binge Wraps Up Chocolate Market," *New York Times*, July 24, 2010, http://www.nytimes.com/2010/07/25/business/global/25chocolate.html.

30 Oliver Nieburg, "Soaring Demand for Sustainable Cocoa Prompts World Bank to Invest $55m in Cocoa Trader," *ConfectioneryNews*, May 9, 2012, http://www.confectionerynews.com/Commodities/Soaring-demand-for-sustainable-cocoa-prompts-World-Bank-to-invest-55m-in-cocoa-trader.

31 Armajaro Trading Overview, 8–9, http://www.sustainablefoodlab.org/wp-content/uploads/2016/01/5.-PCA-Armajaro-Ecom.pdf.

32 For a detailed history, see Beckman, *Organising the Farmers*.

33 Frederick Cooper, *Africa Since 1940: The Past of the Present* (Cambridge: Cambridge University Press, 2002), especially ch. 4.

34 See, for example, James Ferguson's analysis in *Expectations of Modernity: Myths and Meanings of Urban Life on the Zambian Copperbelt* (Berkeley: University of California Press, 1999).

35 "Akuafo Adamfo Hits Significant Milestone," *GhanaWeb*, June 19, 2013, http://www.ghanaweb.com/GhanaHomePage/NewsArchive/Akuafo-Adamfo-hits-significant-milestone-277334.

36 "Special Report: Côte d'Ivoire's Cocoa Sector Reforms 2011–2012," *Agritrade*, December 16, 2012, http://agritrade.cta.int/en/layout/set/print/Agriculture/Commodities/Cocoa/Special-report-Cote-d-Ivoire-s-cocoa-sector-reforms-2011-2012.

37 Dasmani Laary, "Ghana Fixes New Cocoa Price to Control Smuggling," *Africa Report*, October 5, 2015, http://www.theafricareport.com/West-Africa/ghana-fixes-new-cocoa-price-to-control-smuggling.html.

38 Matthew Mpoke Bigg, "Update 2 – Ghana Sets 2016–17 Season Farmgate Cocoa Price at $1914 per Tonne," *Reuters*, October 1, 2016, http://www.reuters.com/article/ghana-cocoa-idUSL8N1C70DK.

39 Olivier Monnier, Isis Almeida, and Baudelaire Mieu, "Ivory Coast Seeks Compensation for Cocoa-Export Defaults," *Bloomberg*, February 6, 2017, https://www.bloomberg.com/news/articles/2017-02-06/ivory-coast-said-to-seek-compensation-for-cocoa-export-defaults.

40 Olivier Monnier and Baudelaire Mieu, "World Bank to Grant Ivory Coast Budget Aid as Cocoa Price Slumps," *Bloomberg*, April 22, 2017, https://www.bloomberg.com/news/articles/2017-04-22/

world-bank-to-grant-ivory-coast-budget-aid-as-cocoa-price-slumps.

5 ECONOMICS ON THE GROUND

1 Vincent Fobelets and Adrian de Groot Ruiz authored the report, available at http://www.chocolatemakers.nl/wordpress/wp-content/uploads/2016/04/TP-Cocoa.pdf.

2 *True Price*, 23.

3 Raviprasad Kamila, "Prices of Domestic Dry Cocoa Beans Slide," *Hindu*, December 26, 2012, http://www.thehindu.com/news/cities/Mangalore/prices-of-domestic-dry-cocoa-beans-slide/article4240514.ece.

4 *The World Cocoa Economy: Past and Present* (July 2012), 14, https://www.icco.org/about-us/international-cocoa-agreements/cat_view/30-related-documents/45-statistics-other-statistics.html.

5 Local prices are from the film *Nothing Like Chocolate*, directed and produced by Kum-Kum Bhavnani (Oley, PA: Bullfrog Films, 2013). I calculated US$ price equivalents based on the exchange rate, fixed since 1976, of 2.70 East Caribbean dollars to 1 US dollar.

6 Gwyneth Fries, Eli Weiss, and Kendra White, *Agro-Logistics for Nutmeg & Cocoa Exports from Grenada: A Logistics Chain Approach* (International Bank for Reconstruction and Development and World Bank, 2013), http://documents.worldbank.org/curated/en/862581468250482805/text/826100WP0P1457720Box379867B00PUBLIC00ACS.txt.

7 Jeff Neilson, Kartika Fauziah, and Alexander Meekin, "Effects of an Export Tax on the Farm-Gate Price of Indonesian Cocoa Beans," paper presented at the Malaysian International Cocoa Conference, October 2013, 5.

8 For details, see chapter 1, note 39.

9 See http://data.worldbank.org/indicator/NY.GNP.PCAP.CD?locations=GB.

10 Janelle Richards, "Chocolate Is a Bittersweet Way of Life in Ghana," *NBC Nightly News*, September 29, 2014, http://www.nbcnews.com/nightly-news/chocolate-bittersweet-way-life-ghana-n212741.

11 US edition, cover.
12 Stephanie Barrientos and Kwadwo Asenso-Okyere, *Mapping Sustainable Production in Ghanaian Cocoa* (2008), 11, https://www.cocoalife.org/progress/mapping-sustainable-production-in-ghanaian-cocoa.
13 See Allman and Tashjian, *"I Will Not Eat Stone."*
14 Stephanie Barrientos noted a similar rationale of physical arduousness for cocoa's male character; see "Gendered Production Networks: Sustaining Cocoa-Chocolate Sourcing in Ghana and India," Brooks World Poverty Institute Working Paper 186 (2013), 7.
15 For an illuminating insight into women's cocoa labor in Ghana, and its intersection with gender norms and reproductive responsibilities, see the video *Gender and Fairtrade – The Stories of Women Cocoa Farmers in Ghana*, presented by the Centre for Development Studies at the University of Bath, https://vimeo.com/154721350.
16 Personal communication, Hannah Davis, January 31, 2017.
17 "Migration, Citizenship and Autochthony: Strategies and Challenges for State-Building in Côte d'Ivoire," *Journal of Contemporary African Studies* 30, no. 2 (2012).
18 "Migration, Citizenship and Autochthony," 274.
19 *Chocolate Nations*, 64.
20 Mitchell, "Land Tenure Reform."
21 "Land Tenure Reform," 210.

6 TRADE JUSTICE

1 For evidence of chocolate's importance as a food ration for Antarctic explorers and researchers, historically and today, see Jason Anthony, *Hoosh: Roast Penguin, Scurvy Day, and Other Stories of Antarctic Cuisine* (Lincoln: University of Nebraska Press, 2012).
2 See https://makechocolatefair.org/issues/cocoa-prices-and-income-farmers-0.
3 Mick Blowfield, "Ethical Supply Chains in the Cocoa, Coffee and Tea Industries," *Greener Management International* 43 (2003), 19.
4 See http://truevisiontv.com/films/details/90/

slavery-a-global-investigation and http://www.kevinbales.net/about.html.

5 Edvard Pettersson, "Child Slavery Claims Against Nestle, Cargill Get One More Chance," *Bloomberg*, January 9, 2017, https://www.bloomberg.com/news/articles/2017-01-09/child-slavery-claims-against-nestle-cargill-get-one-more-chance.

6 Blowfield, "Ethical Supply Chains," 18.

7 These figures and those that follow in this paragraph are from *Child Labor in the Cocoa Sector of West Africa: A Synthesis of Findings in Cameroon, Côte d'Ivoire, Ghana, and Nigeria* (2002), 12–13, http://www.globalexchange.org/sites/default/files/IITACocoaResearch.pdf.

8 Amanda Berlan, "Social Sustainability in Agriculture: An Anthropological Perspective on Child Labour in Cocoa Production in Ghana," *Journal of Development Studies* 49, no. 8 (2013), 1094.

9 Quoted in Ryan, *Chocolate Nations*, 44.

10 International Labor Rights Forum (ILRF), *The Cocoa Protocol: Success or Failure?* (June 2008), 2, http://www.laborrights.org/publications/cocoa-protocol-success-or-failure.

11 Stephanie Barrientos, Uma Kothari, and Nicola Phillips, "Dynamics of Unfree Labour in the Contemporary Global Economy," *Journal of Development Studies* 49, no. 8 (2013).

12 "Dynamics of Unfree Labour," 1039.

13 For example, in early 2017, Mondelēz increased prices for some Cadbury products, citing the rising price of cocoa. While cocoa's price had been increasing for several years prior, the announcement came at a time when it hit a three-year low. See Martinne Geller, "Cadbury Owner Mondelēz Raises Some Prices on Weak Pound, Higher Cocoa Cost," *Reuters*, January 12, 2017, http://uk.reuters.com/article/uk-mondelez-freddo-price-idUKKBN14W2OT?il=0.

14 Details of Berlan's findings are from "Social Sustainability in Agriculture."

15 Allman and Tashjian, *"I Will Not Eat Stone."*

16 See http://www.cocoainitiative.org/about-ici/about-us. For industry partners, see http://www.cocoainitiative.org/about-ici/our-partners/industry-members. For civil society partners, see http://www.cocoainitiative.org/about-ici/our-partners/civil-union-partners.

17 *The International Cocoa Initiative: Strategy 2015–2020*, 1–2, http://www.cocoainitiative.org/wp-content/uploads/2016/03/ ICI_strategy_EN_digital_pxp.pdf.
18 See http://agoa.info/about-agoa.html.
19 See http://www.fairforlife.org.
20 See http://fairtradeusa.org.
21 See https://utz.org. As this book went to press, Utz announced a merger with Rainforest Alliance certification, which focuses on environmental conservation. See https://utz.org/merger.
22 See http://www.fairtrade.net/products.html.
23 See https://www.fairtrade.net/standards/aims-of-fairtrade-standards.html.
24 See http://www.fairtrade.net/about-fairtrade/what-is-fairtrade.html.
25 Fairtrade International, *Monitoring the Scope and Benefits of Fairtrade: Cocoa*, seventh edition (February 2016), fig. 7.15, http://www.slideshare.net/fairtrade/fairtrade-cocoa-facts-figures-monitoring-the-scope-and-benefits-of-fairtrade-7th-edition-2015.
26 See https://www.fairtrade.net/about-fairtrade/fairtrade-sourcing-programs/fsp-cocoa-mark.html.
27 See http://www.fairtrade.net/about-fairtrade/who-we-are.html.
28 See http://www.fairtrade.org.uk/en/buying-fairtrade/chocolate/cadbury.
29 See http://www.nestle.co.uk/csv2013/socialimpact/responsiblesourcing/nestlecocoaplan.
30 Fairtrade International, *Scope and Benefits of Fairtrade*, seventh edition (2015), 91, https://www.fairtrade.net/fileadmin/user_upload/content/2009/resources/2015-Monitoring_and_Impact_Report_web.pdf.
31 See http://www.fairtrade.org.uk/en/media-centre/news/october-2015/fairtrade-certified-cocoa-mars-bars-hit-the-shelves.
32 Marc Gunther, "Hershey's Uses More Certified Sustainable Cocoa, But Farmers May Not Be Seeing the Benefits," *Guardian*, July 6, 2015, https://www.theguardian.com/sustainable-business/2015/jul/06/hersheys-mars-ferrero-cocoa-farming-fair-trade-global-exchange.
33 See http://www.fairtrade.org.uk/en/media-centre/news/november-2016/cocoa-life-and-fairtrade-partnership.
34 Personal communication, Sophi Tranchell, February 24, 2016.

35 Personal communication, Sophi Tranchell, February 24, 2016.
36 I analyzed images from this campaign in "Cosmopolitan Cocoa Farmers: Refashioning Africa in Divine Chocolate Advertisements," *Journal of African Cultural Studies* 24, no. 2 (2012).
37 *Cocoa Barometer 2010*, 12.
38 "Organic Cocoa Prices Not Sufficient Incentive to Stimulate Production," *Agritrade*, January 19, 2014, http://agritrade. cta.int/en/layout/set/print/Agriculture/Topics/Product-differentiation/Organic-cocoa-prices-not-sufficient-incentive-to-stimulate-production.
39 See http://www.icco.org/about-cocoa/chocolate-industry.html.
40 ICCO, *A Study on the Market for Organic Cocoa* (July 2006), 5, https://www.icco.org/about-us/international-cocoa-agreements/cat_view/30-related-documents/37-fair-trade-organic-cocoa.html.
41 For details, see *Taza Chocolate Annual Cacao Sourcing Transparency Report* (2015), 12, https://www.tazachocolate.com/pages/taza-direct-trade.
42 See "Our Direct Trade Program Commitments," https://cdn.shopify.com/s/files/1/0974/7668/files/Taza_DT_Commitments_Aug2015.pdf?2533070453853065353.

7 GOVERNING QUALITY

1 *Chocolate, Women and Empire*, especially chs. 1 and 2.
2 See http://www.tcho.com/shop/chocolate/bars/dark-chocolate-chocolatey-70g-bar-70-percent-cacao-22100. In contrast, Ecuador is "nutty" and Peru is "fruity."
3 See http://www.icco.org/about-cocoa/fine-or-flavour-cocoa.html.
4 Report by the Chairman on the Meeting of the ICCO Ad Hoc Panel on Fine or Flavour Cocoa to Review Annex "C" of the International Cocoa Agreement, 2010, https://www.icco.org/about-us/international-cocoa-agreements/cat_view/30-related-documents/215-fine-or-flavour-cocoa.html.
5 Application and flavor designation process details from Oliver Nieburg, "Premium Chocolate 'Leg Up': How to Win Fine Flavor Cocoa Status," *ConfectioneryNews*, May 10, 2016, http://

www.confectionerynews.com/Commodities/Everything-you-need-to-know-about-fine-flavor-cocoa.

6 For details of the Mesoamerican Criollo–Forastero shift, see Presilla, *New Taste*, 33–8.

7 Motamayor et al., "Geographic and Genetic Population Differentiation of the Amazonian Chocolate Tree (*Theobroma cacao* L)," *PLOSone* 3, no. 10 (2008), http://journals.plos.org/plosone/article/file?id=10.1371/journal.pone.0003311&type=printable.

8 See https://www.c-spot.com/atlas/chocolate-strains.

9 See https://www.c-spot.com/atlas/chocolate-strains/primary-strains/grandiflorum.

10 See https://www.c-spot.com/atlas/chocolate-strains/cultivar-strains/ccn-51.

11 See https://www.c-spot.com/atlas/chocolate-strains/cultivar-strains/porcelana.

12 "A Dynamic Bean-to-Bar Market Creates the 'New American Chocolate' – But Is It a Game for Small Players Only?" *ConfectioneryNews*, October 2, 2015, http://www.confectionerynews.com/Markets/Bean-to-bar-chocolate-rises-in-US-Can-multinationals-join-in.

13 See https://www.c-spot.com/atlas/chocolate-strains/cultivar-strains/chuao.

14 Gwyn R. Campbell, "The Cocoa Frontier in Madagascar, the Comoro Islands and Réunion, c. 1820–1970," in *Cocoa Pioneer Fronts*.

15 For a discussion of the "community" aspect that can develop around single origin chocolate, see my article "'Artisan' as Brand."

16 During fermentation, pulp liquefies and drains away. However, sometimes, cocoa pulp is harvested for use as a flavoring. For example, the Malaysian Cocoa Board uses pulp in fruit-flavored jellies; in Hawaii, Madre Chocolate makes a Triple Cacao bar that includes chocolate, nibs, and pulp; and Claudio Corallo, chocolate maker in São Tomé and Príncipe, has produced confections infused with pulp.

17 Gulustan Ozturk and Glenn M. Young, "Food Evolution: The Impact of Society and Science on the Fermentation of Cocoa Beans," *Comprehensive Reviews in Food Science and Food Safety* 16 (2017), 451, http://onlinelibrary.wiley.com/doi/10.1111/1541-4337.12264/full.

18 "Gendered Production Networks," 18.
19 Personal communication, January 16, 2016.
20 See http://www.tcho.com/tchosource/#partners.
21 Personal communication, Laura Sweitzer, February 17, 2017.

8 SUSTAINABLE FUTURES

1 For example, Mark Schatzker, "To Save Chocolate, Scientists Develop New Breeds of Cacao," *Bloomberg*, November 13, 2014, http://www.bloomberg.com/news/articles/2014-11-14/to-save-chocolate-scientists-develop-new-breeds-of-cacao; Stacey Vanek Smith, "Ecuador's Answer to the Global Cocoa Shortage," *NPR Special Series: Planet Money*, February 19, 2015, http://www.npr.org/2015/02/19/387420709/ecuadors-answer-to-the-global-cocoa-shortage.
2 Anga, *World Cocoa Economy*, 16, 18.
3 Personal communication, January 16, 2016.
4 See https://www.cocoalife.org/the-program.
5 For Hershey, see https://www.thehersheycompany.com/en_us/responsibility/good-business/creating-goodness/cocoa-sustainability.html. For Mars, see http://www.worldcocoafoundation.org/a-taste-for-sustainability.
6 See http://www.nestle.com/csv/communities/nestle-cocoa-plan.
7 For Olam, see http://olamgroup.com/products-services/confectionery-beverage-ingredients/cocoa/sustainability. For Cargill, see https://www.cargill.com/sustainability/cocoa/sustainable-cocoa.
8 See https://www.barry-callebaut.com/sustainability/forever-chocolate/thats-what-forever-chocolate-all-about.
9 Harry Wallop, "The Many Ways Cadbury is Losing Its Magic," *Telegraph*, March 21, 2016, http://www.telegraph.co.uk/food-and-drink/features/the-many-ways-cadbury-is-losing-its-magic.
10 See Jeffrey G. Stern, "The History of CCN-51 in Ecuador," *Chocolate & Cacao Education & Training*, September 13, 2011, http://jeffreygstern.com/ecuadorian-cacao-varieties/the-history-of-ccn-51; and Oliver Nieburg, "CCN-51: Cocoa's Shining Light or a Risky Monocrop?" *ConfectioneryNews*, August 9, 2016,

http://www.confectionerynews.com/Commodities/CCN-51-Cocoa-s-shining-light-or-a-risky-monocrop.

11 Doug Hawkins and Chen Yingheng, United Cacao Limited SEZC report, Hardman & Co., May 11, 2015, 14, http://www.hardmanandco.com/docs/default-source/company-docs/united-cacao-limited-sezc-documents/ucl-initiation-may2015.

12 See http://www.cocoaofexcellence.org.

13 See http://hcpcacao.org.

14 See https://chocolateinstitute.org.

15 Schatzker, "To Save Chocolate."

16 See http://www.ohcf.us.

17 See http://www.lonohana.com.

18 See http://madrechocolate.com/Madre_Chocolate_Hawaii/Home.html.

19 See http://marouchocolate.com.

20 See https://en-gb.facebook.com/Kallari-Chocolate-68963262649.

21 Personal communication, February 24, 2016.

Selected Readings

As will quickly become apparent, thanks to its sexiness and sales potential, the word "chocolate" routinely wins out over "cocoa" in book titles, at least among the English language literature that I reference here. This is the case even when the subject is primarily the latter (the current volume is a rare exception). Many superb cocoa books masquerade as works on chocolate, so it is always worth taking a look inside. That said, if there is a canon of cocoa works, then it certainly begins with the inestimable volume by Sophie D. Coe and Michael D. Coe, *The True History of Chocolate*, second edition (London: Thames & Hudson, 2007), whose impeccable research into cocoa's Mesoamerican history and European transformations set a high bar for all that followed. Among his prolific works, William Gervase Clarence-Smith has produced two detailed volumes that are must-reads for students of cocoa's economic history: the monograph *Cocoa and Chocolate, 1765–1914* (London: Routledge, 2000), on trade expansion, and the edited volume *Cocoa Pioneer Fronts since 1800: The Role of Smallholders, Planters and Merchants* (London: Macmillan, 1996), which provides geographically diverse accounts of exogenous plantings, including locations whose cocoa histories are seldom addressed. Two journalistic accounts, both based on fieldwork at origins, reveal darker industry aspects: Carol Off's *Bitter Chocolate: Anatomy of an Industry* (New York: New Press, 2006) and Órla Ryan's *Chocolate*

Nations: Living and Dying for Cocoa in West Africa (London: Zed Books, 2011). Upon its recent publication, Mara P. Squicciarini and Johan Swinnen's edited volume, *The Economics of Chocolate* (Oxford: Oxford University Press, 2016), immediately improved access to multidisciplinary research on industry economics. The ICCO website, http://icco.org, is also a useful starting point for research. In addition to industry overviews, it publishes daily price information and reports on various trade aspects. The ICCO archives price data only for a limited period, but *Trading Economics* has cocoa prices dating to July 1959: http://www.tradingeconomics.com/commodity/cocoa. *ConfectioneryNews* publishes regular updates on the cocoa and chocolate industries; look particularly for articles by Oliver Nieburg at http://www.confectionerynews.com.

Chapter 1   All of the works listed above informed my introductory framework to this book. Several others have been equally important as I thought through the politicization of cocoa, and how the many actors along its supply chain both wield and contest power through this commodity. Lourdes Benería's chapter, "Gender and the Social Construction of Markets," in *The Feminist Economics of Trade*, eds. Irene van Staveren, Diane Elson, Caren Grown, and Nilüfer Çağatay (London: Routledge, 2007), helped me articulate the social construction of markets. James Ferguson's *Global Shadows: Africa in the Neoliberal World Order* (London: Duke University Press, 2006) gave me an anthropological lens for understanding how racialized representations of sub-Saharan Africa reinforce and maintain its material poverty. Frederick Cooper's concept of the gatekeeper state in *Africa Since 1940: The Past of the Present* (Cambridge: Cambridge University Press, 2002) has long been foundational to my understanding of cocoa's political importance in West Africa. Michael Pollan's analysis of the bidirectional influence between cultivated foods and human behaviors in *The Botany of Desire: A Plant's Eye View of the World* (New York: Random House, 2001) informed my analysis of cocoa's power over people. I was very grateful for access to the ICCO *QBCS*, XLIII, no. 1 (Cocoa Year 2016/17), which provided the most up-to-date and accurate figures for production, exports, imports, and grindings cited in this and subsequent chapters.

Chapter 2   Readers interested in Mesoamerican cocoa cultures should start with Cameron L. McNeil, ed., *Chocolate in Mesoamerica: A Cultural History of Cacao* (Gainesville: University Press of Florida, 2006). Marcy Norton's *Sacred Gifts, Profane Pleasures: A History of Tobacco and Chocolate in the Atlantic World* (Ithaca: Cornell University Press, 2008) reveals the dependency of early European cocoa consumers on indigenous Mesoamerican knowledge. For a detailed cultivation history, see Allen M. Young, *The Chocolate Tree: A Natural History of Cacao*, revised and expanded edition (Gainesville: University Press of Florida, 2007). Among the many topics covered in Louis Evan Grivetti and Howard-Yana Shapiro's hefty edited volume, *Chocolate: History, Culture, and Heritage* (Hoboken, NJ: John Wiley & Sons, 2009), several chapters include examples of chocolate's early advertising and ephemera in Europe and the US. Lowell J. Satre opened the eyes of contemporary students of cocoa to the egregious history of São Tomé slave labor in *Chocolate on Trial: Slavery, Politics & the Ethics of Business* (Athens: Ohio University Press, 2005). Catherine Higgs published another carefully detailed account of the same in *Chocolate Islands: Cocoa, Slavery, and Colonial Africa* (Athens: Ohio University Press, 2012). I drew upon Clarence-Smith, *Cocoa and Chocolate*, for details of slave and forced labor in the Americas and Caribbean, and *Cocoa Pioneer Fronts* for cocoa's expansion beyond Mesoamerica.

Since their publication, Polly Hill's pioneering works, *The Gold Coast Cocoa Farmer: A Preliminary Survey* (London: Oxford University Press, 1956) and *The Migrant Cocoa-Farmers of Southern Ghana: A Study in Rural Capitalism* (Cambridge: Cambridge University Press, 1963), have been foundational to studies of cocoa in West Africa.

Chapter 3 Emmanuel Ohene Afoakwa has produced two comprehensive volumes on manufacturing: *Cocoa Production and Processing Technology* (London: CRC Press, 2014) and *Chocolate Science and Technology*, second edition (Oxford: Wiley-Blackwell, 2016). Though technical guides, both address history and trade, including Fairtrade and organic production. A staple of manufacturers' bookshelves is Stephen T. Beckett's *The Science of Chocolate*, second edition (Cambridge: Royal Society of Chemistry, 2008). Also a technical guide, focused on chemistry, it is a superb reference for semi-finished products and chocolate. Edward George's report for Ecobank, *Overview of Global Cocoa, Coffee and Sugar Markets* (November 2013), which includes West Africa export figures, can be accessed at http://www.globalgrainevents.com/pdfs/Geneva%/202013/EdwardGeorgeEcobankOverview.pdf. Both Ryan's *Chocolate Nations* and Catherine Araujo Bonjean and Jean-François Brun's chapter, "Concentration and Price Transmission in the Cocoa-Chocolate Chain" in *Economics of Chocolate*, are useful for understanding the geopolitics of value added processing. I was indebted to Clarence-Smith's *Cocoa and Chocolate* for the history of cocoa and chocolate tariffs in this chapter. The USITC report on *AGOA* (2014) is available at https://www.usitc.gov/publications/332/pub4461.pdf.

Chapter 4 Several "corporate biographies" bring readers inside the world's largest chocolate companies. As the only journalist permitted extensive access to Mars, Joël

Glenn Brenner offers unique comparisons between the US rivals in *The Emperors of Chocolate: Inside the Secret World of Hershey & Mars* (New York: Broadway Books, 2000). Michael D'Antonio's biography *Hershey: Milton S. Hershey's Extraordinary Life of Wealth, Empire, and Utopian Dreams* (London: Simon & Schuster, 2006), charts the rise of mass-marketed chocolate in the US. A member of the Cadbury family, Deborah Cadbury offers a detailed company history in *Chocolate Wars: From Cadbury to Kraft* (London: Harper Press, 2011). After working for two of the Big Five, Lawrence L. Allen revealed the fierce competition among all of them for market supremacy in China in *Chocolate Fortunes: The Battle for the Hearts, Minds, and Wallets of China's Consumers* (New York: AMACOM, 2010). For a technical account of global industry structure (including futures trading), see Robin Dand, *The International Cocoa Trade*, third edition (Cambridge: Woodhead, 2011). Bonjean and Brun analyze the processing landscape prior to ADM's sales of its cocoa and chocolate businesses in "Concentration and Price Transmission" in *Economics of Chocolate*. In his chapter in the same volume, "The Dynamics of the World Cocoa Price," Christopher L. Gilbert includes a chart of cocoa's price from 1850 to 2013, as well as production and grindings statistics. The ICCO report, *The Cocoa Market Situation*, issued in July 2014, provides supply and demand figures and is accessible at https://www.icco.org/about-us/international-cocoa-agreements/cat_view/30-related-doc uments/45-statistics-other-statistics.html. Gavin Fridell's argument for coffee statecraft in *Coffee* (Cambridge: Polity, 2014) offers a comparison with state cocoa power in Ivory Coast and Ghana. A great deal of work has been published on Ghana's cocoa industry, thanks to its long history, socio-cultural and political economic importance, and unique market structure. Among the most relevant to this chapter are Björn Beckman's *Organising the Farmers: Cocoa Politics and National Development in Ghana* (Uppsala: Scandinavian Institute of African Studies, 1976) for its detailed history of cocoa taxes, and Cooper's *Africa Since 1940* for Kwame Nkrumah's gatekeeping around cocoa revenues. For further details on Ghana's liberalization and COCOBOD's sector oversight, see Stephanie Barrientos and Kwadwo Asenso-Okyere, "Cocoa Value Chain: Challenges Facing Ghana in a Changing Global Confectionary Market," *Journal für Entwicklungspolitik*, 25, no. 2 (2009). These findings came from a study that Barrientos and Asenso-Okyere conducted for Cadbury in 2008; their comprehensive report, *Mapping Sustainable Production in Ghanaian Cocoa*, can be downloaded from the Cocoa Life website at https://www.cocoalife.org/progress/mapping-sustainable-production-in-ghanaian-cocoa. For a clear definition of structural adjustment, as well as feminist critiques of SAPs in several countries (including Ghana), see Pamela Sparr, ed., *Mortgaging Women's Lives: Feminist Critiques of Structural Adjustment* (London: Zed Books, 1994). Diane Elson has challenged the purported gender neutrality of macroeconomic policies; see "Macroeconomics and Macroeconomic Policy from a Gender Perspective," Public Hearing of Study Commission "Globalisation of the World Economy – Challenges and Responses," February 18, 2002, and its bibliography for SAP-specific publications, http://www.cepal.org/mujer/curso/elson3.pdf. Details on Ivory Coast's forward buying and minimum price can be found in Agritrade, "Special Report: Côte d'Ivoire's Cocoa Sector Reforms 2011–2012" (December 16, 2012), available at http://agritrade.cta.int/en/layout/set/print/Agriculture/Commodities/Cocoa/Special-report-Cote-d-Ivoire-s-cocoa-sector-reforms-2011-2012.

Chapter 5 For more information on price, see the

ICCO report, *The World Cocoa Economy: Past and Present* (July 2012), which covers 2002 to 2012 and can be accessed at https://www.icco.org/about-us/international-cocoa-agreements/cat_view/30-related-documents/45-statistics-other-statistics.html. The paper presented by Jeff Neilson, Kartika Fauziah, and Alexander Meekin at the 2013 Malaysian International Cocoa Conference, "Effects of an Export Tax on the Farm-Gate Price of Indonesian Cocoa Beans," provides context for Indonesian cultivation and farm gate price. For a deep dive into revenue and costs along the value chain from farmers to retailers, and an assessment of "living income," see *Cocoa Barometer 2015* by the Barometer Consortium, which can be downloaded at http://www.cocoabarometer.org/Download.html. *Mapping Sustainable Production* by Barrientos and Asenso-Okyere details farmer income in Ghana. A number of scholars have shed light on the gendered dynamics of cocoa production. Barrientos, "Gendered Global Production Networks: Analysis of Cocoa-Chocolate Sourcing," *Regional Studies* 48, no. 5 (2014), examines gendered divisions of labor and income in Ghana and India. Tsutomu Takane's elegant work, *The Cocoa Farmers of Southern Ghana: Incentives, Institutions, and Change in Rural West Africa* (Chiba: Institute of Developing Economies Japan External Trade Organization, 2002), provides fieldwork data on intra-household gender relations and gender heterogeneity in earnings, as well as an accessible account of the share cropping abusa system and tenant farming. Jean Allman and Victoria Tashjian's collaborative history, *"I Will Not Eat Stone": A Woman's History of Colonial Asante* (Portsmouth, NH: Heinemann Press, 2000), documents the impact of expanded cocoa production on women in Ghana. For Ester Boserup's pioneering work, see *Woman's Role in Economic Development* (London: Allen & Unwin, 1970). This chapter's section on sociopolitics in Ivory Coast is indebted to two articles by Matthew I. Mitchell: "Land Tenure Reform and Politics in Post-Conflict Côte d'Ivoire: A Precarious Peace in the Western Cocoa Regions," *Canadian Journal of African Studies* 48, no. 2 (2014) and "Migration, Citizenship and Autochthony: Strategies and Challenges for State-Building in Côte d'Ivoire," *Journal of Contemporary African Studies* 30, no. 2 (2012). Both offer robustly evidenced accounts of migration's role in the Ivorian conflict. Ryan also addresses the history of this conflict in *Chocolate Nations*, chapter 2, as does Off in *Bitter Chocolate*.

Chapter 6   Readers interested to learn more about the causes and impacts of unfree labor, including child labor, should start with Stephanie Barrientos, Uma Kothari, and Nicola Phillips, "Dynamics of Unfree Labour in the Contemporary Global Economy," *Journal of Development Studies*, 49, no. 8 (2013). See also Mick Blowfield, "Ethical Supply Chains in the Cocoa, Coffee and Tea Industries," *Greener Management International* 43 (2003). The ICI makes a great deal of recent research on child labor in Ivory Coast and Ghana available at http://www.cocoainitia tive.org/knowledge-centre/ici-reports. The International Programme on the Elimination of Child Labour provides background context and survey findings on child labor in West Africa in "Combating Child Labour in Cocoa Growing" (2005), available for download at http://www. ilo.org/public//english/standards/ipec/themes/cocoa/ download/2005_02_cl_cocoa.pdf. The ILRF report on the Harkin-Engel Protocol, *The Cocoa Protocol: Success or Failure?* (June 2008), can be accessed at http://www.labor rights.org/publications/cocoa-protocol-success-or-failure. For investigations of West Africa's regional migration and child labor in cocoa farming, see Off, *Bitter Chocolate*, chapters 6 and 7, and Ryan, *Chocolate Nations*, chapter 3.

I drew gratefully in this chapter upon Amanda Berlan's ethnographic account of children's farm labor in Ghana, "Social Sustainability in Agriculture: An Anthropological Perspective on Child Labour in Cocoa Production in Ghana," *Journal of Development Studies*, 49, no. 8 (2013). For further background, scope, and statistics regarding Fairtrade cocoa, see Fairtrade International, *Monitoring the Scope and Benefits of Fairtrade: Cocoa*, seventh edition (February 2016), available at http://www.slideshare.net/fairtrade/fairtrade-cocoa-facts-figures-monitoring-the-scope-and-benefits-of-fairtrade-7th-edition-2015, and the Fairtrade cocoa page at https://www.fairtrade.net/products/cocoa.html. For details on the US market, see Fair Trade USA, *Fair Trade Certified Cocoa Review 2010–11*, available at https://fairtradeusa.org/sites/default/files/Cocoa_Impact_Report.pdf. For a critical review of Fairtrade, see Amanda Berlan and Catherine Dolan, "Of Red Herrings and Immutabilities: Rethinking Fairtrade's Ethic of Relationality among Cocoa Producers," in *Food Transgressions: Making Sense of Contemporary Food Politics*, eds. Michael K. Goodman and Colin Sage (Farnham: Ashgate, 2014). For a history of the relationship between Kuapa Kokoo and Divine Chocolate, see http://www.divinechocolate.com/uk/about-us/research-resources/divine-story and Bob Doherty and Sophi Tranchell, "New Thinking in International Trade? A Case Study of The Day Chocolate Company," *Sustainable Development* 13 (2005). For details on the founding of Kuapa Kokoo within Ghana's liberalized market, see Pauline Tiffin, Jacqui MacDonald, Haruna Maamah, and Frema Osei-Opare, "From Tree-Minders to Global Players: Cocoa Farmers in Ghana," in *Chains of Fortune: Linking Women Producers and Workers with Global Markets*, ed. Marilyn Carr (London: Commonwealth Secretariat, 2004). More information on organic cocoa can be found in Tropical Commodity Coalition, *Cocoa Barometer 2010*, available for download at http://www.cocoabarometer.org/Download_files/Cocoa%/ 20Barometer%/202010.pdf; ICCO, *A Study on the Market for Organic Cocoa* (July 2006), available at https://www.ic co.org/about-us/international-cocoa-agreements/cat_view /30-related-documents/37-fair-trade-organic-cocoa.html; and Fair Trade USA, *Fair Trade Certified Cocoa Review 2010–11*. *Taza Chocolate Transparency Reports* from 2011 can be downloaded at https://www.tazachocolate.com/pages/ taza-direct-trade. *Dandelion Chocolate Sourcing Reports* from 2014 can be downloaded at http://www.dandelionchoco late.com/our-beans.

Chapter 7 For readers interested in fermentation and drying, the ICCO provides information at https:// www.icco.org/about-cocoa/harvesting-and-post-harvest. html. Technical details can be found in Afoakwa's *Cocoa Production and Processing Technology* and *Chocolate Science and Technology*. For a meticulous (and illustrated) discussion of cocoa quality and cultivation in Mesoamerica, see Maricel Presilla, *The New Taste of Chocolate*, revised edition (Berkeley: Ten Speed Press, 2009), in particular, "A Natural and Cultural History of Chocolate." For information about the ICCO Ad Hoc Panel on Fine or Flavour Cocoa, visit http://www.icco.org/about-cocoa/ fine-or-flavour-cocoa.html. The study by Motamayor et al. on new genetic classifications, "Geographic and Genetic Population Differentiation of the Amazonian Chocolate Tree (*Theobroma cacao* L)," *PLOSone*, 3, no. 10 (2008), can be downloaded at http://journals.plos.org/plosone/article/ file?id=10.1371/journal.pone.0003311&type=printable.   I discuss the equation of quality with consistency for mainstream brands, in contrast to flavor distinctions of single origin chocolate, in "Invisible West Africa: The Politics of Single Origin Chocolate," *Gastronomica: The Journal of Critical Food Studies* 13, no. 3 (2013). For a history of Criollo cultivation in Madagascar, see Gwyn R. Campbell's chapter, "The Cocoa Frontier in Madagascar, the Comoro Islands and Réunion, c. 1820–1970," in *Cocoa Pioneer Fronts*.

  Chapter 8   For information about production trends and supply predictions, see Jean-Marc Anga's ICCO report, *The World Cocoa Economy: Current Status, Challenges and Prospects* (April 2014), which can be accessed at http://unctad.org/meetings/en/Presentation/SUC_MEM2014_09042014_ICCO.pdf, and ICCO, *World Cocoa Economy* (2012). Pam Williams and Jim Eber advocate for the flavor bean approach to sustainability in *Raising the Bar: The Future of Fine Chocolate* (Vancouver: Wilmor, 2012), as does Simran Sethi in *Bread Wine Chocolate: The Slow Loss of Foods We Love* (New York: HarperOne, 2015). For an assessment of sustainable production in Ghana, see Barrientos and Asenso-Okyere, *Mapping Sustainable Production*.

Index

Pages where figures appear are *italicized*; pages where tables appear are in **bold**.